MURDER ON THE HO]

It's a Ferry story.

Rob Little

Also by Rob Little

The Jock Connection on the Trail of the comic
Billy Bagman

The Life of Riley and His Troubles

Scratcher in the Wry

Humour Bawdy and Blue
from the Rob Little Cellar

In memory of Patricia, my loving wife of fifty years, and for Susan, Dawn and Louise, my cherished daughters, and my every bit as special grandsons Christopher and Guy.

A donation from every book sold goes to Nith Inshore Rescue and the RNLI

Copyright Rob Little 2024.

All persons mentioned in this publication are fictitious and any resemblance to persons living or dead is coincidental.

FOREWORD

In 1940, Rob was born in Cardiff. His grandfather was Scottish, but both of his parents were Welsh born. In 1941, Hitler bombing all parts of industrialised Wales, the family moved back to the village of Ruthwell in Dumfriesshire, Scotland.

From 1961, Rob served in the British Merchant Navy, working as an electrician. He sailed to those faraway places with strange sounding names, faraway over the sea, honed his chat up lines using outrageous patter, flirting with any Sheila or Judy, having girls chortling uncontrollably at his mirth.

Entertainment for ship's crews, whilst at sea, in those days, was listening to BBC broadcasts on short wave radio and the chronic, deafening, ear-offending squelch. Having the urine extracted by a fellow crewmember was an ever-present danger. Rob, too, had a talent for that form of amusement, which you can detect in his writing.

In the 1960s Rob had a short spell in London's Met Police. The call of the sea strong, Rob succumbed to the call. During his 18 years of ferry service he sailed from Dover and Felixstowe to the Continent and from Cairnryan to Larne in Northern Ireland.

Rob would like to point out that the characters in this book bear no similarities whatsoever to any person, male or female, still living or still dead, he met during his days as a merchant seaman, or in his long and varied life; the characters and storyline, set in the days before 'Brexit', are a fabrication of his imagination.

Chapter 1

December, on any of London's Metropolitan Police divisions, was the month of the heavily laden shoplifter and the obstreperous drunk. Cases increased tenfold as did court appearances and the overtime bill, even for 'out-in-the-sticks' divisions. Detectives on any Met division were rarely involved with this category of offender, the Met classing both offences as minor crimes. On the more law abiding divisions beat plods thought any arrests a big deal. The uniformed branch had the duties of arresting drunks found in a public place, their prosecution and of shoplifters previously arrested by store detectives. All ranks were happy.

Detective Constable Hamish Macnab found time to spend with other plain-clothed coppers, in the pub that locals knew as The Rozzers Arms, playing pool, supping beer, Guinness his tipple, noshing pork pies, any make, scotch pies being hard to find. Curries, vindaloo his favourite, were always free to coppers on the mump from various outlets on the manor. Card games, where he gambled loose change, he hoped to win a copper or two from the less-card-astute aides to CID.

That December the serious crimes perpetrated on their subdivision had involved detectives of various squads but not a team that affected Hamish and his boozing colleagues. Pub Christmas clubs, in which drinkers had put money by all year to buy their festive booze, hadn't received the attention of local hoodlums. Cash returned from banks to pubs had arrived safely, usually with a visible uniformed presence guarding. The licensees delivering a free pint or two to the guards at their back doors; the reward delighted the plods, with the hope their guv'nors never knew about the drink. Coppers now in promoted ranks would have also received the tipple for similar services but would never admit to it.

Hamish enjoyed pubs as much as he did detecting crime. Sitting, relaxed, back to a wall, at a table in the Rozzers, with his plain clothed oppos, he still had the mind-set to respond quickly to a shout if one came in. It was late in the month. Festive revellers still chased the 'hair of the dog'. Christmas had passed. He looked forward to Hogmanay three days away.

His inspector pushed aside the pub swing doors, strode into the busy bar, stopped, his eyes casing the gloom, fixing on the table of 'his finest'. Looming over the table, he placed his hands onto it, moved a pile of cards and coins to one side and interrupted the afternoon session.

We have a 'shout' was Hamish's first thought as he saw the inspector raise a crooked finger and summon him to a private spot, tear him from his colleagues midst. Hamish left a half-eaten pie laid on the card table. The cards dealt to him he carried with him and slid them into a pocket; his oppos had history of sneaking a peek, cheating when the opportunity arose.

Divisional commander Jack Dewsnap wanted to see him in his office.

His inspector said, taking Hamish outside onto the quiet of the pavement, 'It sounds as if the commander wants you to go undercover on a job. It might be a bit like the service you had successfully performed for him a couple of years ago with Harry MacSporran, but I've no idea what. He wants to see you today. Better be on your way. You know how crabbed and testy he's been lately.'

He told the inspector, 'I'd better play this hand and pay up, the cards are poor. Then I'll be on my way. Shouldn't take long.'

During the years, from first reporting for CID duty at the Divisional Headquarters, Hamish had seen the commander on his weekly visits to the subdivision nick to which he had attached him. The commander never appeared cheery. His demeanour kept coppers out on their beats. Bitter of face, storming like a tornado, he had marched like a demented drill sergeant through all departments and the canteen, a pain in the ear and the backside of the entire sub-divisional strength. The faults he found were usually trivial, the lower ranks getting the worst shouting at. He stared closely at unshaven faces, pointed at hair lengths, and shoddy dress sense. He spat with rage at young beat coppers if he found rumpled creases on their uniform trousers, unpressed shirt collars and boot toecaps poorly bulled.

He hadn't wish anyone seasonal blessings again this year.

Rumours that had circulated, in recent months, repeated with bated breaths by divisional strength, suggesting that his wife, Daphne, had left him, his marriage in tatters, had proved correct.

Hamish had pondered on the marriage break up, keeping his thoughts to himself. He and Detective Constable Harry MacSporran were the only coppers at the sub-division, and perhaps the entire Met Force, knowing of the commander's presence in that Gent's toilet, and what had happened, in that cubicle, on that year's Halloween blind date. When Jack met incognito with Daphne, both wearing Halloween masks, neither knowing who the other was, at the time.

Hamish thought that Commander Dewsnap would never want the traumatising event revealed. Had Daphne learned that husband Jack was the person who met her outside the park gates on that blind date? She, too, would never want that knowledge revealed or how she had acted with the masked man, unknown to her that night.

The commander had kept his promise of promotion back to Detective Constables, for he and Harry MacSporran, on completion of their successful 'hush-hush' detective work in finding a comedian's gig he could take his wife to, her deal with him to have her return to the marital bed, in that part of the manor known to the police strength as the Irish Quarter or the IQ. The now retired copper William Beckam, who was moonlighting as that comedian, Billy Bagman, was now a class act and appearing each summer in a Blackpool theatre and each winter in Benidorm bars.

He and Harry had settled back into detecting crime, prosecuting criminals, loved the thrill of putting them away, ridding the streets of their presence. Various crimes needed investigating on the division. Their detection rate was excellent whatever squad their inspector had attached them to. Arrest numbers were mounting, adding to their Jock Connection nickname renown. Both Hamish and Harry thought the commander should be nothing but impressed with their mounting tally.

Hamish hitched a ride in an area car to the Headquarters. He looked his scruffy self as he mounted the stairs to the division senior officers' offices. He was unshaven since Christmas Day. Clad in tattered leather jacket, ill-fitting T-shirt, Jeans and Tuff boots, he wiped a hand over his hair as he knocked on the commander's office door.

The less you looked like a cop, the less chance villains had of noticing they were under observation, his argument.

If the commander had wanted to give him a bollocking for his appearance, he had the perfect answer.

'Sit down, MacNab,' the commander said as Hamish entered the office, no friendliness in his voice; only a throaty gruffness, much as it was the last time the commander had summoned Hamish had cause to appear in front of him. Hamish pulled up a chair, positioned himself in front of the desk so he could look the commander in the eye.

He thought the commander didn't look any healthier this time round, the bags beneath his eyes blacker. He could not recall ever seeing anyone with wanker's doom, slang words often used in British prisons for inmates guilty of excessive masturbation. He hadn't heard or ruminated over the saying since his youth in Govan. It was one way that summed up the commander's facial appearance. His face also had a tormented twist to it, his bottom lip sagging, as if he'd gone to bed the night before a committed Freemason, which he was, and had awakened in the morning believing he was the chief warlock of a Barking coven and had lost his magical powers. He had cast off his uniform jacket, hung it crookedly over his chair back, his clip-on tie hung on a wing of his shirt collar and dangled beneath his neck.

When Hamish settled himself in the chair, the commander spoke, 'I've been looking through the CVs of detectives on the division. I found in yours the experience and qualities necessary in a detective for this wee job. It's an undercover investigation. You'll be delighted with it. Suits you, as they say.'

Leaning forward in the chair, Hamish looked the commander straight in the eye and erupted, 'You'll not get my warrant card off me so easy this time.'

He knew well the hard-to-stomach conditions attached to the 'duties elsewhere' investigations he and Harry had conducted in the Irish Quarter for the commander when they had to investigate without their warrant cards in their possession.

'No need this time. This is a legit case. I have permission right from the top. Before you joined the Job you were at sea. In the British Merchant Navy, I take it?'

'Aye,' Hamish replied.

He was wondering what next was coming out of the commanders mouth.

'Well, how do you fancy going back to sea for a ferry trip or two, be onboard for one week?'

'I wasn't happy with my demotion from detective constable to uniformed constable, the pain of trudging around foot beats or my transfer to this division. I could easily have chosen a return to seafaring then. I was pleased that you needed me and my partner Harry MacSporran to go undercover to find you the comedian Billy Bagman. You promised the restoration of our detective rank and kept it. I'm happy now. It's working well for you. We're doing our bit to keep divisional arrest numbers up. My wife also thought she detected a notion I had of drifting back to sea. She certainly put the anchors down and expected them to hold fast when she told me she was expecting twins. I've a son and a daughter now. I won't be travelling too far in the near future anyway.'

'Reminding me of that undercover work you did will get you nowhere with me, MacNab,' the commander snapped, his face souring, his eyes narrowing, giving Hamish a look of contempt as the aftermath of the Halloween blind date resurfaced. 'You began as a scullion, I see here.

What's that?' The commander spat out as he flicked open a file and drew a finger down the A4 page under his gaze.

'It's the lowest of the low. Toiling in the ship's galley, peeling spuds, cleaning pans, humping stores, hosing down the deck. Being at the cooks' beck-and-call,' Hamish said, his brow furrowed.

He was still wondering what was coming next.

'Then you were a seaman's peggy, then a steward and then second cook. Was this on deep sea ships?'

'Aye. I did five years. I went away when I was sixteen. All the trips I did were with a shipping company that British seamen knew as Hungry Hogarths, proper title the Baron Line. They were a Glasgow tramp company, known throughout the merch for their allegedly poor feeding, long trips, and low wages. I tramped round the world three times. I sailed with all sorts of characters, saved a bob or two.

'I had my cook's ticket by the end. Like an idiot, I came ashore, got married. I wasn't happy in Civvy Street. I couldn't settle. I couldn't rid myself of the call of the sea. The call is real. Life was hell. That's what brought me to the Met. I've found happiness as a detective detecting crime, arresting criminals and taking them to court.

'Nowadays, things have changed at sea. The British Merchant fleet's diminished to cruise ships, tankers, huge container ships all with Asian crews and reduced manning, and the ferries. British seamen have become a rare sighting. As a Tory voter, you'll think that the unions, the docker's and seamen's, with their militancy and strikes, ruined the normal cargo shipping business?'

The commander moved forward in his chair, rapping of his fingertips on his desk, speeding up as he said, 'Aha, a bolshie. Just what's needed, that's if it takes one to know one? You'll probably not be aware that, in recent months, a ferry has started trading from Ballymagilligan, a small port in the Irish Republic, to the port of Holyhead on Anglesey?

'Haven't seen or heard of that service. Dover and other channel ports, Hull, Felixstowe, and Cairnryan up in Scotland I have. Ferry companies are major seagoing employers nowadays. That doesn't mean it's good news for British seafarers seeking work. Ferry company management will already know of the cheap labour available from Thailand, the Philippines, India, Bangladesh, with Romanians getting in on the act, too. With a cook's ticket I might have had the chance of a job on one and been happy back at sea,' Hamish answered.

The commander looked up from the sheet. 'The father of the managing director of The Holigan Ferry Company plays golf with Deputy Assistant Commissioner Beaverton on Sundays. That's how word of this first came to The DAC's notice. 'Crewmembers on board the ferry, Holigan Express, are militant, dangerous rabble-rousers. Dishonesty is rife. Crewmembers steal food. The MD suspects crew are fiddling in the passenger bar.

'A purser the MD employed died. A crewmember found him in his bunk when he didn't appear for breakfast. Medics, when they arrived onboard, tried to revive him. He was too far gone. Oxygen starvation they said the cause. An autopsy seems to suggest that the man died of suffocation. From a comment made by a crew member the Gardai thinking is that he croaked between the bodies of the two large stewardesses working onboard. On their trips off, the women are known to give sexual gratification, servicing the needs of the affluent male Dublin community. Maybe they have form providing that level of service, advertise the fact. Perhaps Gardai have been partaking of the service, maybe caught at it. Who knows? They've not parted with that info.

'A trace of semen suggests he was trying to pleasure one of them at the time. The other woman was pressing him on to greater glory, nibbling his ears and urging him on from the back by the sound of it, waiting to change her position. Perhaps the positional change killed the purser if he was that lucky. A sandwich, I've heard the experience called.'

The commander placed the A4 sheet in a folder and said, 'This is of more interest, to the Met and me, anyway. The world has become smaller in terms of illicit product availability. It was no surprise that about the same time as the DAC heard about the thieving, the Irish Gardai contacted the Met. They've long suspected that organised crime gangs are using ferries to move illegal immigrants and drugs.

'It's a lucrative business. Known organised crime gangs are moving in, both on the mainland and in the Irish Republic. All news channels are reporting the spike in people trafficking. It's essential for police forces to work together and learn what crimes we can investigate jointly and effectively. We're still in the Common Market but for how long I don't know. Rumour has it that we'll be out next year. Drug squad commander consensus is that the pooling of resources will allow us to be more efficient, disrupt and prosecute criminal gangs working in Ireland and over here.

'Tackling organised crime, in partnership, is a key part of policing, everywhere in the civilised world. It's the job of all police forces to stay ahead of these criminals. Your introduction onto the ferry will prove that a strong working relationship can exist between the Gardai and the Met. We can hope it will be to the detriment and the punishment of any criminals using the ferry, in both directions, as transportation for drugs and illegals.

'I've been chatting with a Dublin Gardai commander. The Gardai know that the two stewardesses on board the ferry are daughters of a small-time Dublin gangster whose operation they want to take a look at to see in what way he's involved. The women may not be entirely honest, not dangerous to men, not murderesses, oversexed and on the game. They could be following orders. The purser who died might have refused to follow their criminal wishes, cut their overtime payment. Who knows?

'We will expect you to learn something about their onboard activities. I don't want to hear reports of you caught in a sandwich as the filling and destroying a bunk during a heavyweight entanglement.' The Commander raised a hand and coughed into it, had difficulty stifling a laugh, his face relaxing, a short-lived smile creasing his face.

He was recalling the devastation of Mayor Algernon Rideout's bed, when his wife, Myrna, had invited Hamish and Harry into the Mayoral boudoir for a sexual romp, rumpy pumpy unlimited.

'And if you happen to get your end away with any of them,' he continued, 'for heaven's sake wear a condom. The Met has had enough problems with undercover officers blotting their copybooks, leaving sprogs behind, then scarpering, the mothers never hearing from them until nosey, investigative journalists revealed their identity.

'Gardai detectives of their drug and people trafficking squads are investigating whether criminals are using this ferry and the ports it uses as gateways through which to import and export their merchandise.

'The investigation is in its infancy. The company MD knows nothing of the Gardai suspicions. The Gardai commander thinks, whilst your remit onboard is to suss out crew thieving, your main focus should be to detect crimes upon which they can act, leading to arrests onboard and ashore, here and in the republic.

'I have a small mobile phone to take with you. The two numbers registered in contacts will get you through to the Gardai commander's office and to my private number. The Gardai commander has the prefix +353. Use the Gardai number, whilst in Irish waters, for immediate back up or reporting anything of significance. Use my number any time, day, or night for the same reasons. Think of a number and use it as a password to protect the mobile so others cannot use it if stolen. Keep it safe. Remove the sim card. It's small and easier to hide until you need to use the phone.

'When you're conversing with me or the Gardai and anyone's eavesdropping, make out, if you can, that you're talking to your mother. I'll be mother. We'll work out certain code words and their meanings before you join the ferry or soon after.

'The Gardai murder squad detectives were about to board the ferry and interview the women about the purser's death. However, since learning of the likelihood of your arrival on board, they've cancelled that, hoping you will suss out what is really going on onboard Holigan Express. As well as working as stewardesses the women might be also selling their bodies onboard, who knows.

'You are the right person to step in, give our Irish cousins the aid they seem to need. You will fit in seamlessly. You've the seagoing experience and in this division's Irish Quarter. You will know Irishisms, a little of Irish peccadilloes. I could not find a role for your partner MacSporran; however, criminal activities on our streets will keep him busy. I've checked and you have no court cases needing your presence in the one week you're away.

'The general feeling of the Gardai officer I've spoken to is that crewmembers will remain tight-lipped. They'd tell them nothing useful. They want you to snoop around. Look for anything blatant without drawing suspicion on yourself. They want evidence and names of those suspected of aiding drug running or people trafficking. This undercover situation is right up your street. The company office is on Holyhead harbour. The managing director, Fred Fields, would like *his* problems sorted so he can make a profit from onboard sales.'

As the commander updated on Gardai suspicions, Hamish wondered why *he* was again putting his trust in his good friend Rowley Beaverton, the person who had set up the abortive, Halloween blind date for him and his wife. This made him ask, 'How are you going to slip me on board a ferry, without me being recognised as a cop?'

'It's convenient that you join the ferry next Wednesday. A second cook is taking extended leave during that period. His wife is pregnant and apparently near her time. The company needs a temporary replacement. That's you. Apparently, short period reliefs are quite normal in their leave system. The ferry's registration port is Piraeus, in Greece. I don't know the details you might have to provide. The MD said you would need a discharge book. If you have one, take it with you. You might have to sign on articles, whatever that means. I take it you will still have the book?'

'It will be at my mother's home in Glasgow. I'll have to pay a visit and get it. I doubt my galley gear will fit me now, be a tad tight. I hope the marine outfitters on the Broomielaw are still in business.'

The commander said, glancing at Hamish, 'You have the stature of a cook. He lowered his eyes and locked them on to Hamish's girth. 'You love food by the look of you. You don't look any slimmer than last time you sat in front of me. I agree you'll need new gear,' he said, his eyes moving up and down over Hamish's overhang and the strained belt holding up his jeans. 'You'll still have an idea how a ship works, the hierarchy, who's who. You'll sign on as a second cook, using your own name. The purser on board the ferry for the fortnight is also a Jock. His only other company employed Asian crews so could never have bumped into you. This is his first trip in the company and on ferries.

'The company have no other Jock employed on board the ferry. The crew are a mix, from Wales, the Northwest of England but mainly Irish. No employee in the company has a London address or has a CRO file. I'm confident no one will recognise you. If anyone does recognise you or suspects what you are, leave the ferry at the next port and travel quickly and safely away. Take no chances. Stay safe.

'According to the MD, the job requires no exceptional culinary skills. So long as you can carve and dice meat, peel spuds, cook frozen chips, prepare veg, fry an egg and flash off a steak, you'll pass muster. The only person on board who will know whom and what you are will be the captain. He doesn't know that you are also snooping for the Gardai. It's a one week tour of duty. I expect you'll be able to spot any fiddling going on, allowing the MD to sack the thieves, prosecute them, if he wants to, and suss out any major criminal activity before your tour ends. I recommend that you make a readable account of interesting occurrences. You know what I mean. You don't have to make it pocketbook style, but I suggest you put an account on the mobile, where necessary put day, date, time and place I saw, etcetera, and save it, just in case you need to give evidence in a court case.'

Hamish thought, on hearing the mention of a storyline, he would include details of any salacious incidents, inflame them, make them sound more interesting, without compromising himself. Those tales his squad mates would enjoy when he returned, even if the commander wouldn't.

He thought the commander would love details of an incident from his earlier seagoing life. On hearing the tale, he might hope they would happen to him whilst he was on the ferry. He moved his butt, leaned forward, threw out his arms and said, 'One stormy night, in the middle of the Pacific, the skipper of a deep-sea ship that I had signed on as second cook went missing. An investigation didn't prove anything. We galley staff couldn't be sure, but we suspected that members of the deck crew knocked him on the head with an empty rum bottle and tossed him and the bottle overboard, aft, onto the propeller, cut to pieces by the blades, because he cut their beer ration, which seamen see as a crime. I wouldn't like anything like that to happen to me.

'The ship turned to look for him next morning. No one saw him, or any part of him, bobbing about in the oggin. Six types of shark circled the ship. They all looked nasty and hungry. If the propeller blades didn't finish him off then the sharks would. The ship sailed on. The local force investigated when we arrived in the next port, but nobody could prove that the skipper hadn't filled his pockets with heavy steel shackles, was suffering depression, and jumped.

'I don't suppose I'll be on danger money, so I'd better watch my step and be careful. I'll take my stick with me,' Hamish said, and sat back in the chair.

The commander eyed Hamish and said in a raised voice, 'Come on now. Looking at your weight, it would take twenty strong men to lift you over the ship's rail and dump you in the Irish Sea? Get yourself home, MacNab. Don't worry. Square it with your wife. Take a train or a flight to Glasgow. Book a flight from Glasgow to Dublin for next Wednesday morning. Take a taxi to the port. The ferry should dock around 2pm. Get receipts. Put in a claim when you return. I'll make sure you're compensated for any expenditure, but don't take the piss.

Hamish took his wife Jenny and the twins with him by train to his mother's home, in Govan, Glasgow. He hadn't spent a New Year in Scotland for five years. He enjoyed the festivities, family banter, the supping of malts, a pint of Tennent's lager and took in an Old Firm game at Ibrox.

Chapter 2

WEDNESDAY AFTERNOON.
BALLYMAGILLIGAN HARBOUR

Rupert Sewell stood shivering beneath his blue gaberdine coat as he watched the ferry approach Ballymagilligan Harbour. It was a cold, early January afternoon in the Irish Republic. The rising wind quickly reddening Rupert's nose, cheeks, and ears, was also frothing the tips of waves rolling up the narrow inlet; heavily and loudly, the waves were crashing into the quay wall, spray flying into the air and over the top. Fishing boats, riding the waves, unstably made for the fishing port further up the inlet to discharge their catch.

Wednesday was crew changeover day and Rupert awaited the berthing of the ferry Holigan Express. He knew the vessel he was joining as purser traded between the harbour and the port of Holyhead in Anglesey.

Rupert had managed to get a seat on a late morning Edinburgh to Dublin flight. A taxi from Dublin airport took him to the harbour. It was his first visit to the Irish Republic; indeed, in his seagoing life, he had sailed with engineers and deck officers from Ulster, but seldom with any person of officer rank from the Republic, and never with crew: the company he worked for during his earlier seagoing career employed Asian crew: Goanese.

Rupert was wearing a cap, known by merchant ship crews as an officer's steaming bonnet. Fixed to it was the HOLIGAN FERRY COMPANY cap badge of blue and gold crossed anchors. The badge gilding flashed occasionally, reflecting rays of the low sun on its rare and fleeting appearances through darkening clouds. Rupert had travelled by train from Waverly Station in Edinburgh, on a cross-country route, for his interview with the ferry company. His train had taken him via Carlisle, and he had to make sure it stopped on its way south at Warrington Bank Quay, for a connection to Holyhead. Fred Fields, the ferry company Managing Director, had handed him the badge on employing him.

Parts of the morning interview, two weeks before Christmas, in the company office, on Holyhead harbour, had rattled Rupert. Fred Fields was ruddy of face and dressed casually; shirt wide open at the collar, sweating a bit with the heating turned up, he sat opposite him across a table strewn with paperwork. Fred had said his piece to him, in a rambling, hiccup-strewn, slurring voice, as if he'd been drinking.

Rupert had furrowed his brow as he listened, got the gist of what Fred said about wearing the badge with pride, that they were a new ferry outfit intending to expand, become a dependable passenger and freight ferrying company, using established ports, creating new ones around the UK coast and on the island of Ireland.

That the ferry on the run did two round trips in twenty-four hours. The crossing from Holyhead breakwater to the berth in Ballymagilligan is over sixty miles and the ferry struggles to do fifteen knots. Each Saturday the ferry missed the overnight sailings and had a 'lay over' in Holyhead until Sunday night when it resumed the schedule. Weekends, when freight trade fell off, the engine department had time to do maintenance they couldn't undertake on the run, which the main engines and auxiliaries needed. The ferry had clocked up thousands of sea miles in her day. And if trade continues to build up, he'd charter another ferry and create a service to the continent. That he formed the company name using beginning of Holyhead and the end of Ballymagilligan, which reflected their first venture into ferrying, but eventually it would become a popular name in the European roll-on roll-off freight and foot passenger trade, become a respected rival to both P and O Ferries, Irish Ferries and the Stenna Line.

Fred's words, You will earn wages, leave and conditions that you could only have dreamt of during your career as a purser on deep-sea ships, sold him on taking the position.

The salary and conditions of service offered pleased Rupert. He would spend the same time at home on leave as he would aboard a ferry.

However, Fred's following statement perturbed him and he remembered his words well. Rupert, we expect you to run a tight and disciplined hotel infrastructure aboard our ferry. Low exchange rates mean it's too costly buying stores from the republic. Holyhead based chandlers supply most catering requirements and spirits for the bar. Irish Republic chandlers supply kegged beer and Irish stilled drinks to the ferry. Passengers and crew cannot access duty free goods whilst we're still in the EU.

We have to make profits in the cafeteria and bar. The profit percentages aren't right. Sales don't reflect the passenger numbers we carry. I'm sure crew are fiddling in these areas. It will be a major part of your duties to discover how they're doing it and to end it.

You can sack them, he said, thumping the table loudly, spittle flying from lips that he wiped before carrying on his spiel. You will get my full backing. I will not tolerate theft; he had said louder still and again thumped the table. His voice hadn't quietened when he said, 'the onboard feeding-rate is away too high. The crew and officers must think they're on daddy's yacht. I'm informed that both officers and crew can order a sirloin steak for their evening meal, when we give them a perfectly good menu to choose from. Who eats sirloin steak seven nights a week for their dinner, even in these less-austere days?

He sounded subdued when he said, The present purser isn't doing enough, not a company's man, too soft, I think. I took him on in haste, as I did with other crewmembers, when we started the run. The purser you're replacing, Hugh Rice. Early reports we've had say he had a heart attack and died.' He bowed his head when he said, 'I expect to attend his funeral sometime soon. A younger, experienced man, like you, will do a proper job for us and make the cuts and savings in these areas. You'll have to be tough, show strength, take nothing lying down. Your degree in hospitality and experience as a purser since graduating will have honed your mind to end all these goings on in your domain onboard Holigan Express, and to keep up our level of service to passengers and crew.

The British Merchant Navy deep-sea fleet had diminished in size over recent decades. Its downsizing had contributed to Rupert's redundancy from the deep-sea company that he'd worked for since his first trip to sea. He'd been happy sailing to the Indian sub-continent and down as far as Cape Town and other South African ports, for twenty-five years, on general-cargo ships that carried twelve passengers, until containerisation grabbed the freight and planes the passengers.

Rupert felt chuffed that reemployment had come quickly after the job loss. He had not relished the thought of working ashore, managing a hotel, but had no idea what ferry life would be like; how he might combat the fiddling, the waste, or the lavish feeding rate that had so wound up Fred Fields. Working with 'white crew' for the first time he thought would be interesting. He had found the Goanese honest and diligent workers.

Rupert, forty-four, broadly built but not overweight, still had a head of black hair, no grey showing, black eyebrows, and a black facial growth when he didn't shave daily.

His blue eyes always seemed to be looking up at other people. His height of five-foot six-inches tall had never troubled him.

The flat cap firmly seated on his head didn't make him look any taller.

That afternoon, the cap's secure seating had prevented the repeated cold blasts snatching it away; gusts that he noted were increasing in ferocity and veering in direction as he stood looking over the inlet. He guessed the wind already had a high Beaufort scale number, and a severe storm was threatening.

Seabirds were soaring higher, heading inland, their squawks lost on the wind. Sheep on the hillside across the inlet herded together. The clump of their black faces, looking across towards the harbour, stood out against the greenery, gorse bushes and heather clumps.

The steam funnelling from Ballymagilligan power station, sited a kilometre up the inlet from the harbour, the wind was flattening to speeding clouds. Rupert knew that such a rising wind and sea forecast a bumpy return voyage to the Welsh coast.

He thought the harbour looked barely adequate to run a successful ferry service. He could see no brick buildings, no regular reception for ticket issue, for passengers or freight. A comfortable waiting area with a cafeteria and other facilities he thought necessary to improve passenger footfall. A couple of horseboxes, articulated lorries of different lengths and half a dozen cars had parked in lanes, waiting to cross.

Two Tugmasters, unaccompanied freight trailer towing vehicles, stood near a portacabin positioned against the wall that surrounded the harbour. A sign fitted above the portacabin door said in large lettering HOLYHEAD FERRY BOOK HERE. It was the only sign of the service. It didn't compare with the small, though modern, shoreside office and reception in the busy port of Holyhead.

As Rupert stood, he watched a taxi pull onto the harbour and stop nearby. He noted the six-foot tall man stepping out of it carrying a holdall. The man wore a heavy sheepskin coat and had the bulk to fit into it neatly. The man looked around and spotted him. He began walking towards him with long strides. As he neared, Rupert thought for a moment the man looked a bit like Desperate Dan of the comic: he had such a square jaw and the build. He wondered if the man would speak with a Scottish accent: as a child, he always thought the comedic, cow pie eating Dan a Scot.

The man did speak with a Scottish accent when he asked, 'Are you joining the Holigan Express?' and stuck out a hand in greeting.

Rupert removed a glove and shook the hand. 'Yes, I'm Rupert Sewell. I'm joining as purser. And you are?'

The cap, which seafarers knew as a steaming bonnet, was the only visible sign that Rupert was an officer. The man could have noticed that. The navy-blue gabardine coat, well buttoned up against the cold, hid his

18

uniform and the three gold braids of rank circling its jacket cuffs.

'I'm Hamish MacNab. I flew down from Glasgow this morning. I'm joining as second cook. It's been a while since I was at sea. It will be good to get back.'

Rupert replied, 'This will be my first trip on a ferry. I flew down from Edinburgh this morning.' He had wondered if the company would continue paying air fares, thought he'd put MacNab in the picture and said, 'I cannot see the company flying us over here for every duty spell. I think it will be a train journey to Holyhead, if we don't drive, and at our own expense. Conditions and wages are excellent. They'll pay out expenses as per our agreements. I don't yet know what that might be but we should get our flights reimbursed this time.'

Rupert noted individuals, all wearing heavy coats, walking onto the docks to huddle together close by. He thought women stood amongst them, their collars the highest; they all protected their faces similarly. He said to Hamish, 'That looks like some of the crew arriving.'

Hamish looked round and said, 'I think you must be right, Boss. I'll use Boss when I speak to you onboard. I'll mosey over and speak with them. Wouldn't look good me getting cosy with an officer, would it?'

Rupert smiled and nodded his head, but his gaze lingered on the assembling crewmembers. Two hefty females were dancing around, trying to keep their feet warm. He wondered what the women might look like facially.

He thought, if the company employed female crewmembers onboard, they must be Irish; might be as beautiful as the young, dark-haired, and dark-eyed colleens that he'd heard of but had only ever seen in films like The Commitments. Then he considered that employment in Dublin and other major city boutiques were the choices most lookers would make. Skivvying for a ferry company would hardly entice an attractive woman.

A vision of Sophie, the wife he'd left behind in Portobello, flashed into his mind.

Sophie worked as an industrial chemist in a petroleum-refining complex, across the Firth of Forth from Edinburgh, near Grangemouth. She was still a comely woman, whom he cherished. A little fuller of figure these days, like himself, he still found her alluring and had got him up, when he thought of her sexily.

Changes had occurred in her sexual needs but his had not. He had to do without, his frustration irking him but under control.

In the weeks spent with her in their Portobello home, since his deep-sea job ended, he'd found her standoffish. Her words and actions made it abundantly clear to him that she'd no wish to allow him to make love to her. A fleeting peck on the cheek the closest she'd come to him, out of bed, or in, when his view of the not-to-be-lifted nightie covering her back had become the norm.

Her social life had become a bit set and never included him. It irked him that the Scrabble club she'd joined took her out most evenings. Her meetings with the posh ladies of the Stockbridge Scrabble Brigade, or the SSB, she called them, and their visits for matches with other women's organisations, as far afield as Biggar in the west, Penicuik and Peebles in the south and Inverkeithing across the Forth road bridge to the North, were of greater interest to her than socialising with him or having 'yon', sex.

She wanted him to understand that 'yon'---the word she stretched out as if she was saying 'yawn' when she said it, to add importance to it---was out of the question. 'I will not be appearing baggy eyed, tired and distracted, when playing competition or practicing with my friends, which I'll be doing most nights after getting home from work,' was her way of explaining the change.

'Yon' was a favourite word of his mother's. For her it meant 'that' as explained in dictionaries of old-Scottish words. He wondered why Sophie used the word when she had no love for the sex *act*.

Sexual deprivation wasn't the norm when he and Sophie first met.

Sophie had just turned eighteen, he in his early twenties, when she was a passenger travelling with her parents to Mumbai, on the ship he was the purser. Her father was taking up an appointment as an investment manager with a Scottish bank.

Sophie had eyed him up for the most part of the early voyage. From when they met before leaving London Docks and across the Mediterranean Sea her eyes locked in on to his whenever their paths crossed. When she felt the temperature rising, as the ship entered the Red Sea, she'd almost begged him for sex, grabbing his hands and dragging him to a shady spot when walking in the dark on deck. He was young, fit, strong, available, willing, fancied her strongly and had bowed to her every whim. So many positions described in the Karma Sutra did she know, and which he performed with youthful gusto, after he'd succumbed to her charms. He thought she'd lived in India all her life, rather than being on her way to the country for the first time. The book of sexual positions a friend had lent her she had committed to memory, it seemed.

On starlit nights, bright moonbeams streaking the placid Red Sea, the Indian Ocean, and the Bay of Bengal, they'd secretly meet behind the poop deck accommodation, the aromas of ghee, curry spices and fried onions wafting over them from the crew galleys ships of that class had fitted aft. They'd had sex to the beat of the propellers thrashing the water to froth beneath their own foamy bodies. Once they even had applause from the Goanese cooks viewing the couplings from their after-deck accommodation. Of course, the cooks had kept the meetings secret. Boss could cut their overtime.

He'd met her ashore often during regular and lengthy dockings at Mumbai. He liked better the longer periods, occurring during the monsoon season, when the persistent rain could disrupt the discharge and loading of cargo.

They'd fallen in love. Four years later, Sophie with a degree in industrial chemistry (from a Mumbai University), the family returned to Scotland. They were married soon after and she'd sailed with him, as his wife, on voyages, a perk the company allowed their officers.

From her voyages as a passenger, Sophie knew what life would be like at sea and had said loudly and excitedly what her expectations were of ocean-going travel as his wife. 'Rupert, you will take me over all the world's oceans. It will be like endless cruising. On days of cloudless skies, when the sea is like a mirror, we will look for flying fish skimming the surface and pods of dolphins playing around the ship. We will see a lonely albatross following us.' She said. Those words had sounded so romantic then. They had loved each other to bits. He was sure of that.

Then she fell pregnant with their daughter, Morag, now twenty and at university, training to be a primary school teacher. The idyllic life, Sophie had so prized, ended.

Rupert saw the handshakes, heard the backslapping and raised voices that drifted across from the crewmembers gathering. The 'How about yehs?' he heard, the standard vocal greeting. 'To be sure, everything was fine. Got my hole regularly at home for a change,' the reply that created the loudest responses. Rupert assumed they were joining the same ferry that afternoon. All were trying to rub heat back into their hands. He also heard the clink of glass bottles rattling together when a crowd member whom he couldn't see placed a bag onto the ground:.

In view of what MD Fred Fields had said about bar sales, it interested him what they might be. It concerned him how that crewmember might use them: personal consumption or if it were a bar person, a fiddle.

Were other officers present amongst them, he wondered. Rupert thought they would, like he was, be showing respect for their rank by wearing a uniform and a steaming bonnet. He had always joined his earlier company's ships wearing full uniform; they insisted that officers did. Rank and its respect had been everything then.

As his taxi pulled up, Rupert had noticed the brown-hulled ferry with white superstructure and green funnel billowing smoke, rounding the headland. It then set a course from the headland between the mainland and a small island, the low edges of which he could see jutting out into the inlet a good kilometre from the berth. Now the ferry was on a central course and nearing the end of the channel that had buoys with light atop, dancing wildly in the storm-tossed sea, marking shallow water to that side of the inlet. Dead Slow Ahead, it entered the harbour. The crowd were all looking towards the ferry's slow approach.

He assumed it was the Holigan Express. He couldn't make out the name on the bow but guessed it would be docking shortly with the nearby single-deck vehicle ramp.

Although he was twenty paces from the huddle of crewmembers, Rupert heard clearly a man ask, in a rough brogue, 'Is he a chocolate doughboy, or what?' Rupert heard the raised, raucous guffaws and tinkling giggles from his fellow bystanders.

Rupert knew he was short-arsed, that the gabardine didn't flatter his physique but he didn't know about whom the crew were directing their query. Quickly, though, he realised the accents of the men were unlike any he'd ever heard. Not the quiet, cultured, Dublin-speak of the newsreaders and other personalities from the Republic appearing on British TV news channels and shows. The voices he was hearing were unrefined. They had an out-on-their-own gruffness, works-in-progress destroying vowels.

He had picked up simple words of the Asian crew's singsong languages, which were enough to issue orders they understood. Would that ability help him understand the Irish accents he'd hear or Gaelic, whilst working on the ferry, he wondered?

The ferry was the Holigan Express. It passed by, slowed, stopped, and began its turn. Steaming-bonneted officers stood on a bridge wing looking over the side, checking position and the tidal flow. The captain turned the ferry one-hundred-and-eighty degrees. The bow then angled towards the quay.

Rupert assumed the captain would bring the bow to close with the quay.

Seamen on the foredeck would first throw the Turks-head-knotted end of a line ashore. The men assembling on the dock, at a bollard further forward of the ramp and from where he was standing, would grasp it. They would then haul ropes ashore and make them fast. Another mooring gang, waiting to secure the aft ropes, shivered close to the vehicle ramp. The ferry secured alongside, its stern doors would open, the ramp lower and settle to its operating position, to allow the discharging of cars and lorries.

Holigan Express's funnel smoked blacker as the ship's propeller action increased, churning up the mud beneath its keel, to colour the water with brown silt. Screwing itself alongside with main engines and bow thruster wasn't moving the ferry any closer to the quay.

Rupert had no knowledge of local conditions. The tide seemed to be ebbing at a rate of knots from the upper reaches of the inlet, which he noticed broadened significantly further inland. The wind that had veered again and was now blowing strongly off the quay. He still didn't suppose the conditions were going to prevent the ferry berthing.

A seafarer in the huddle obviously thought differently and began another noisy rant, which Rupert's ears were sharp enough to decipher. 'It's that fecken' eajit skipper Dithery Dai. He's havin' yun o' his shite haemorrhages again. He'll piss off oot o' here an' faff aroond ootside till the wind drops and the ebb slackens, afore he puts her alongside, so he will. He does my feckin heid in, so he does, but.'

Ship's officers sometimes referred to signed-on crew of seamen, catering staff and engine-room greasers as 'the crowd'. This crowd were certainly aware that their captain, Dithery Dai, had experienced earlier docking problems. The captain duly gave up his docking attempt and headed back down the inlet. Each crowd member picked up their baggage and trudged off in the direction of what Rupert saw was a pub, outside the dock gates, on the opposite side of the street.

Rupert took the handle of his wheeled case and followed on behind the crowd. The crowd chose the public bar as their venue; he chose the lounge. He ordered a coffee, a sandwich and sat alone, reading his newspaper. He was sure the crowd would tumble out, when the ferry reappeared, their leaving telling him that Dithery Dai had managed to berth her to the ramp and he could go onboard.

Chapter 3

Two hours later, the ebb water flowing from the inlet slackening. Skipper Dithery Dai made a successful docking.

Rupert trundled his suitcase back towards the ferry, looking for a gangway to its upper decks. He couldn't see one. He saw crewmembers and dock workers walking over the ramp. He followed. Stepping off the ramp onto the deck, he stopped, stood still, taking in what he saw. The lighting wasn't good, fluorescents lamps blackened with diesel smoke, shone dimly. He could make out a narrow track marked PEDESTRIANS that crossed the vehicle deck centrally from ramp to a midship structure, where, he guessed, he'd find a staircase leading to the upper decks.

Cars had already begun their exit from the upper vehicle deck down the internal ramp onto the lower deck. Black, acrid diesel smoke was erupting from revving lorries, drivers starting up engines, whilst dockers removed the shackles anchoring them to the deck, getting them ready to roll off.

Crew pushed past Rupert as he stood looking around. He let them walk ahead of him. He stood aside to let a car exit. The driver lowered his window and stuck his head out. Rupert read the words, which hissed from the man's mouth: 'Feckin bollox that you are!'

The act and the words stumped him. Later that afternoon he learned that Tony Ferdie, the purser he was taking over from, was to blame. He'd announced over the PA system, as the ferry neared the berth the first time, 'All drivers must now go to their vehicles ready for disembarkation,' and hadn't recalled them, leaving them lurching and apprehensive in their vehicles, on the vehicle decks, during the docking delay.

Rupert found the purser's office in the small, circular foyer that had illuminated gaming, cigarette and beverage machines fixed to its walls. A door led to a quiet passenger lounge overlooking the stern, a door to the side was marked Officer's Saloon, another to Officer's Accommodation. A grill covered the hatch of the Purser's Office. He saw movement behind it through the gaps. He found the office side door, upon which he knocked, then opened, stepped inside the office, pulling his case behind him.

'Rupert Sewell,' he announced and reached to take the hand offered by the shortish, grey-haired, wrinkly-faced man in civvies.

'Ru, Ru, Rupert. Tony Ferdie,' the man replied, raising his eyebrows, 'pleased to meet you. I've been itching to get off. Bloody useless skipper couldnae lay hissel alongside his missis in bed, without needin' a tug to nudge him intae the lee o' bum island, tae be sure.'

Rupert caught the gist of Tony's rant and asked, 'Have you far to go to your home?'

'A wee place called Naas, a mile or two up the N7 from Dublin. Horsey country it is. That wife o' mine will hae been waiting in the car for me since the clown on the bridge failed in his first attempt. Worried that he'd clatter the quay, no doubt. Bridget will no' be best pleased.'

Rupert unbuttoned his gabardine, slid it off his shoulders, hung it on the hook he noticed behind the door and placed his steaming bonnet on top. He looked around the cubbyhole of an office, and beyond to the cabin that would be his home for his week onboard. He spotted the three-quarter-size-bed. It was low down, safer if you were in danger of high seas jettisoning you onto the deck and would sleep two adults comfortably.

In his early days at sea, high, narrow bunks were the order of the day, set atop three deep storage drawers. He was pleased to see he had his own shower and toilet facilities. Washing and toilet facilities for junior ranks back then was a sink. He believed it was a handy feature for the desperate or plain lazy to walk along the alleyway to the communal toilet and shower area. He had mused often at a story all first trippers heard in the days of poor personal facilities and took time to learn was a wind up: you did not urinate in the sink unless you had a company contract.

Tony said, 'the personnel officer told me this is your first trip on a ferry. Now the first thing we always do on joining is to check the safe. It holds takings and till receipts from the bar and cafeteria, the remnants of the cash float and foreign currency. Holyhead office send staff onboard to empty the bandits and replenish the machines. A different clerk will board for the takings, leaving an updated float.' He hunkered down to the safe, sited beneath the desk. Removing a bunch of keys fastened to his trouser belt, he opened it, withdrew a large cash box, and said, 'You'll have to check that it's correct and we'll both sign the book.'

Rupert checked the cash box contents with Tony and verified them correct. Tony gave a derisory sniff as he rose from the chair. He had noticed, for the first time, and thinking it bullshit run riot, that Rupert's three gold-braided rings circled his uniform jacket cuffs, not the two and only halfway-round braids on his jacket cuffs.

Looking away with a derisory shake of the head, he pulled open a drawer, pointed at a pile of books laid inside and said, 'You'll find an order book for all the stores you'll need, for the bar, cafeterias and the galley.

We've to order all catering requirements in Holyhead. At the present exchange rate, the Republic's too expensive.'

Tony must have thought that advice completed the handover. He slapped the bunch of keys into Rupert's hand and said, 'Best of luck. See you in a week's time.' He then scratched his head, as if he were trying to remember if he'd forgotten anything. Deciding not, he picked up a holdall, then left the office, in a hurry.

Rupert knew that his job as a purser aboard a ferry had to involve duties other than what Tony Ferdie had quickly explained to him.

He tugged his case into the bedroom and lifted it onto his bunk. He checked mattress comfort, that the duvet cover and sheets were clean, fresh, newly changed, then returned to the office.

He removed a clip of notices hanging above the desk to browse. They included a crew list and a duty roster for the catering, waiting and bar staff, his main responsibility. He assumed that returning crew would know their stations. Any new starts would appear soon to sign-on ship's articles, something he'd have to do, if kept onboard and he found them.

A wall-mounted telephone allowed communication with officer's cabins and various other positions. He noted the microphone for the PA system. A dial phone on his desk showed a shoreside phone line existed. He assumed it needed a plug-in connection on dockside, but no one had told if it connected in the Republic. He picked up the handset but heard no burr as he put it to his ear. He saw a typewriter and pile of blank menu cards in a corner, alongside a computer that he thought also needed a shoreside connection to get online.

Rupert started pulling open drawers. Hidden away beneath the order books and ledgers, he found a stash of soft-porn magazines. He was removing the pile for later viewing but changed his mind when a knock disturbed him and a man a wearing short, white, working overcoat entered the office. 'Afternoon, Boss, I'm Alf Roberts, Second Steward,' he said, with a slight slur, 'everyone has joined that should have joined,' and handed him a sheet of paper listing crew names and ranks.

Alf had a drink in him. Rupert could tell that from his speech, the smell of his breath and a little unsteadiness. He had heard reports that, since The Herald of Free Enterprise capsized off Zeebrugge, certain ferry companies banned their crew from drinking aboard; indeed, companies were breathalysing the crew before allowing them to board. Fred Fields hadn't instructed him what the orders were on the Holigan Express. He thought he'd have to find out.

'You're new in the company, Boss?'

'My first day, Alf. You're a Taff, by your accent?'

'One or two of us on are employed on here, isn't it. Welsh crewmembers along with others from the mainland change over in Holyhead. Us Taffs know our place. You might find other crewmembers a bit bolshie, militant-like, hard to deal with, push you for everything they can get. As soon as we sail, they'll all rush here with their expense claims for joining.

'None of them will be happy if their money isn't here for them to piss up against the dock wall in Holyhead on Saturday night. It's your job to vet the claims if you didn't already know. The company is never happy to pay out too much, isn't it.

'Someone in the office sussed out the fiddle a while back. They checked bus runs, the fares and the times buses called at stops closest to every address of those employed on here, isn't it. Now the crew only get bus fares, not taxi fares. Upset lots of expenses cheats, it did.

'You'll find a book detailing what and how often in a year each crew member can rightly claim, which you'll have to scan well, because the best of fiction writers employ the fiddling art on here. They're not all Scousers. You'll find out who they are soon enough. Beware, isn't it!

'You'll want a walk round, before the lorry drivers and passengers get onboard, though it's a quiet for all vehicles and walk-ons. It must be the time of year. I'll introduce you to the catering staff that are on duty and show you the cafeteria, the bar, galley, the passenger cabins and point you in the direction of the storerooms. What do you think?'

'I got all that, Alf. I can see you're going to be a great help to me on here,' Rupert said. 'Let's go, show me around.' He wondered if all Taffs ended their sentences with the words isn't it?

Chapter 4

The galley, cafeteria, crew, and driver's cabins were down a deck. On the rounds with Alf, Rupert found that the cafeteria servery and the passenger bar hadn't yet opened. The cafeteria had a hatch from the servery through to the galley. Meals were deliverable by cafeteria staff to passengers. He noticed the till position and that had no CCTV camera scanning it. He thought to detect any dishonesty at the till the company should fit one, to show the transaction, recording it, later a responsible company employee viewing it and ticking it off as correct. It was something he noted for passing on to the MD, if he was serious to cut out any fiddling that existed.

In the bar, which was at the forward end of the passenger area, with window portholes looking out over the ferry bow, he noted through the bar grill the range of drinks. The bar offered two of each main spirits on optic, cans of beer and soft drinks in a cooler and Harp Lager, Guinness, and Magner's Cider on tap.

He noted the box of straws that covered fully the till screen facing the passenger side of the bar. Very convenient, he thought, if fiddles were in operation: the bar staff placing the cash in the till, wasn't registering it, but pocketing it later, the ferry company only receiving the amount recorded on the till roll. The MD's. fears could be correct. Now, it seemed, the MD. expected him to prove it. His brow furrowed thinking of the difficulties involved verifying any theft, the acrimony the bar person might feel about any improvements he suggested, if he wasn't a dishonest person.

Back in the office, ready to open and address any passenger needs, a rapping on the door alerted him. The door opened. Standing looking in was a bald man, smaller than he was and rotund, a Michelin man, about five-foot four inches tall, wearing a spotless white boilersuit and a sly grin that Rupert thought was phoney, his eyes circling, looking over his head. 'New purser?' the man asked in an Irish accent.'

'Rupert Sewell,' he replied.

'Ru, Ru, Rupert,' the man said, hesitatingly, 'I'm Bo Boyle, second engineer,' he said, breaking into a broader grin, 'but on here I sometimes get Bo B. Has anyone told you about your chief cook?' Bo asked, throwing back his head. Rupert thought Bo must be pointing the back of his head in the direction of the galley. He also thought Bo didn't realise the implication of the nickname that sounded like 'Boaby'. In Scottish slang, his mates or the lassies knowing him as Wee Boaby, he might find upsetting.

Rupert didn't put him wise, but responded, 'I looked into the galley. The cooks wore proper attire. Both were busy preparing our dinner and passenger meals at the time. I'm sure the food they were preparing will be tasty and wholesome enough for crew and passengers. I certainly detected an appetising aroma.'

'Well, I've just walked through the galley. I caught chief cook, Flick Fleck, picking his nose, whilst preparing food. I'm day-work on here, responsible for all mechanical maintenance and need to visit the galley to inspect machinery, like the slicer and the spud peeler. I saw Flick tunnelling a finger deep into a nostril, withdrawing a burrowed bogey, inspecting the extraction lying tacky and covered with scooped-out nasal hair on a fingernail, then flicking it expertly to stick with wonderful adhesion onto a galley bulkhead.'

Seeing signs of disgust wax across Rupert's face, Bo added a disturbing possibility. 'What would you think if the cook mixed the result of a nostril excavation in with his culinary preparations?'

Rupert screwed his face up at the thought.

'He's a rare cook. He dishes up a tasty and spicy curry on a Friday, so he does. Bejasus don't sack him till you get one better,' Bo said. Then he continued, his face contorting into an even wider grin, the likes of which Rupert had never seen. It looked as if Bo were about to describe an enjoyable experience. And he was.

'Saturday nights we don't sail,' he said, 'you know we lay over in Holyhead. It was rare night ashore last Saturday. I laid pipe with a girl known to the locals as the Mamog with Lipstick. Mamog, I've heard, is a female sheep in the Welsh language. Hot ones with fleecy thighs the likes of her live over the water, just waiting for you to part the whiskers. They're not all ugly stumpers needing a bag over their heads and one over yours when you give them one.

'I can get an Anwen or a Blodwyn to throw their body under you if you want. Get one to rid you o' any dirty water lying about your belly, to pump your bilges if they're high, to be sure. And if you like a late drink, I can recommend a lock-in joint. The last Saturday night the ferry was laid over I got back from the pub at three on Sunday morning more pissed than a nursing home chair, but'

Rupert was thinking that Saturday night might have been an enjoyable experience all round for Bo. But it wouldn't be a night to remember for him. Then the office telephone rang. He stuck out a hand towards it.

Landing on the handset, he picked up and brought it quickly to an ear. The diaphragm rattled and from the depths of the earpiece, a coarse, loud, lengthy and resonating raspberry blasted out. Rupert turned the handset smartly away, grasped it with his other hand and prodded his ear with an index finger.

Bo's attempt at chuckle smothering failed. Rupert didn't question Bo on who the offender might be. If he were to believe his reaction, the exaggerated grin on his face, he knew the identity of the phantom raspberry blower.

He didn't want to show he was irked, didn't want Bo to know if he thought the rasping offensive, humorous or humiliating. He casually replaced the handset, turned to face him, and asked, 'Internal telephones on here have faults, do they, dial wrong numbers, are guilty of sending squelch down the line?'

'Not that I'm aware of, Bo replied, his smirk waning, 'you'd better have a word with Screwfix.'

'Screwfix?' Rupert asked, his brow furrowed, 'who might that be?'

'Screwfix is the electrician when you can find him.'

'He's that busy fixing things, I take it. This looks an old ship. Maybe he does need to carry a tool kit, shifting spanner, pliers and a set of screwdrivers around with him; what Electricians I have sailed with said was all they needed to get the ship around the world.' Rupert said.

'Work it out. Screwfix is his nickname. If he's not fixing something he's screwing or looking to. Your best chance of catching him is when the passengers board. You'll usually find him in the foyer or down in the passenger bar, eying up any talent. He's at it here or in Holyhead, daytimes or nighttimes, mornings or afternoons. That's electricians for you. He does more screwing than fixing. He certainly gets to pull and entertain more fanny than me on here,' Bo said, his voice rising, a finger pointing downwards, 'because I've to be down the noisy, oily, smoky, smelly engine room continually, hard at work, out of play, not eying up the talent.'

Shame for you, thought Rupert. He looked for signs of oil and grime on Bo's boilersuit that suggested hard graft but found none.

*

The ferry sailed late Wednesday afternoon. Rupert didn't notice Screwfix in the foyer looking for talent. Was he working for a change?

Holigan Express was pulling away from the berth when a gong sounded in the officer's saloon, which he had spotted just off the foyer, summoning the officers to dinner.

Alf reappeared. 'This is when I take over from you, boss. I just sit and field any enquiries. Anything I can't answer I note down and tell punters to return in an hour and a half. That ok with you?'

'Fine by me, Rupert replied, 'I suppose I'll get into the way things work on here in a day or two.'

In his bathroom he washed his hands and straightened his tie.

Entering the saloon, he saw Bo sitting with officers he hadn't met. All had soup bowls in front of them. Bo was lashing salt and pepper into his. Passing the cruet set along for others to partake of their seasoning needs, he saw Rupert and waved him to the table. Waiting until he'd sat down, Bo then introduced his table companions.

'This is Toots MacAvoy, 3rd Engineer,' Bo began, tapping the engineer sitting next to him on the arm.

'Toots. Is that a common Irish name?' Rupert asked, without levity in his voice.

'No, no,' said Bo and began his explanation. 'It's short for tooting for he's the horniest fecker on here, aren't you, Toots, have the permanent horn, haven't you? Next to him is Rory Pike, fourth engineer. The thin, shagged-to-a-taper beanpole on the end with the wisp of muff diving gear sticking to his chin is the world-famous Screwfix. He gives Toots a run for his money in the shagging stakes on here. To be sure, they're a horny pair of fanny hounds, I can tell you,' Bo said. 'And if Screwfix can't fix it, he'll fuck it, isn't that right, Screwfix?'

Screwfix didn't answer, just smiled wryly, whilst tittering sibilantly.

They seemed an easy-going bunch. Rupert thought he'd easily fit in on the ferry. From their accents, the engineers were all from Ireland.

The conversation that kicked off between them, Rupert expected to be on any subject other than crows.

'I'll tell yeh about crows,' Bo said, his soup bowl empty, 'they're getting ready to breed early this year, but. I've heard their raucous cackling coming from fields under the plough. I've seen them carrying worms and gubbing them when settling on a branch. They're building up strength for the tredding season ahead. It's louder now from the treetops. They're preparing to 'lay pipe' high in the leafless branches, I tell you. Missis Crow will be spreading her legs and getting the old corbie knob thrown up her quite soon, if those happy sounds are anything to go by, but.'

The term laying pipe, a derogatory description of the sex act, wasn't new to Rupert. Now he knew the saying was alive and understood in Ireland.

'Does the Irish crow lay more pipe than the English crow, but?' Rory asked.

'Aye, and as the Irish crow flies, comparing it to its English relative, how much later does an Irish crow suss winter's over and their thoughts turn to the old tredding, but?' Toots asked.

Bo, replying, laughter erupting, addressed Rupert and said, 'If Irish crows are anything like our Toots and Screwfix, then they'll be tredding all the year round. They'll overrun Ireland, the bloody things; we'd have black-plumaged shitehawks everywhere, joining in with the seagulls to cover our pavements white with droppings.'

Rupert thought the engineers and the electrician looked to be in their late twenties. It escaped him why they were interested in the feathery variety of bird, made-up bleaters, and why they grinned at Bo's words. As he was thinking, he noticed they were all looking over him and smiling in unison towards something or someone to his rear.

Rupert looked round to see a stewardess hovering with a dishtowel over her arm. He thought her a big lump of a girl, in her late twenties and one of the females standing with the crowd ashore waiting to board. She smiled at him from a round, friendly face, half seductively hidden by black, wavy hair that had fallen forward; a face that he found attractive. She looked well-built and a looker.

'This is the lovely Cara,' said Bo, 'she'll look after all of your wants in here, breakfast, lunch and dinner she's always about. And she does a grand job of the cabins, too. Make somebody a good wife one of these sweet days, so she will. Isn't that right, Cara, but?'

Cara was blushing slightly, but no more than that. Rupert thought she'd would have suffered banter and wind-ups from the male crewmembers.

Smiling, he looked up at her and said, without looking at the menu, 'I'd like a bowl of soup, please, Cara.' He watched her glide away, then he pulled the receptacle holding the typed menu card towards him across the table.

Bo said quietly, to quiet sniggering from other table guests, 'She'd ride the pointed end of an anvil to destruction, that one!'

Rupert thought the menu was of more interest. He noted an entrée, a main course of roast silverside of beef, a choice of cold meats and salad in season, a sweet with cheese, biscuits, and coffee to follow. It was much as he'd expected and adequate: what he had provided on the deep-sea ships he'd served on. It seemed within range of any respectable company's feeding rate for officers or crew.

When the soup arrived, he thought it looked and smelled delicious, the first slurp exciting his taste buds, creating the thought that the cooks could at least make a palatable pot of broth between them. He had put aside Bo's assertions on Chief Cook Flick Fleck's habits, but his opinion changed when he broke the bread roll into pieces. About to smear the parts with butter, he saw, nestling towards the roll's centre, a small, black, gelatinous mass with short hairs protruding. A crow! Howked from Flick Flecks......................

Convinced that this was a mining from the chief cook's report-worthy nostrils, as reported by Bo, Rupert felt his stomach lurch. He grasped his napkin, held it close to his mouth, pushed his chair back with a clatter, stood up, made muffled apologies to his dining companions, and left the saloon, his stride lengthening.

The explosion of riotous laughter that followed Rupert's hasty departure increased to a sidesplitting frenzy before he was out of earshot. Bo had removed the cause of Rupert's nauseous attack from the bread roll and returned it to the small, clear plastic packet marked Daft Jokes, Incorporated in Ireland.

As the laughter erupted, Rupert realised the raspberry was just the start of pisstaking he might have to endure as a new boy. He had been irked enough by the nonsense to feel his stomach turning but he composed himself, re-entered the saloon in time to see Bo pocket the small packet. He sat down in front of the soup and roll he'd left and said with a wry smile, 'You boys like your pepper and your wind ups. Thought I was about to sneeze over the lot of you. Couldn't let that happen. It's not hygienic and is out-of-place in the officer's saloon. Bo, you'll have more jests like that up your sleeve, I bet,' he said, pointing a finger at Bo's pocket.

Trying not to look hurt, he looked round to see Cara standing, a hand in front of her face, trying hard to suppress a grin. He handed her the plate with the with the roll bits on it and asked, 'Would you please fetch me a fresh roll and a clean plate, please. This roll has had a borrowing alien dig its way into it?'

The ferry had reached the head of the inlet and was about to turn onto its heading for Holyhead. Rupert heard loud voices behind him. He turned his head, followed the gaze of the engineers sitting opposite him. Two men with four rings of braid on their cuffs had entered the saloon to take a round table in a corner of the saloon. Both men looked to be in their late fifties, both entirely grey-headed. They had to be the skipper, the Dithery Dai of the crewmember's rant and the chief engineer.

'I don't know what you expect my engines to do for you, skipper,' the chief engineer was saying as he studied the menu card. Rupert twigged from his accent that he, too, was Irish. 'I gave you all the power I could within the safe temperature limits of the engines' exhaust gasses. To give you any more revs could cause untold damage to my engines. If temperatures go off the scale, pistons and their liners could crack and I have no spares. Even for an emergency double ring of the telegraph, I couldn't give you more revs. If you want me to fuck my engines, get it in writing from head office, but that could mean weeks in port laid up waiting for spares and the heavy work undertaken by dockyard fitters at a fearsome price for the company.

'The company only got off the ground six months ago. They chartered the ferry from the Greeks. It came with few spares. The engineering superintendent is busy contacting breakers' yards all over the world looking for serviceable, main engine parts. My principles wouldn't change if we had new engines. Just get it right on the bridge. Don't ask for what I cannot give.' His tirade over, the chief handed the menu to the captain.

'I needed more power from the engines in the weather and tide conditions we had today, during my first attempt to get alongside the quay, isn't it. And the bow thruster isn't doing much, either is it?' the captain said, whiningly, 'not pushing the bow around at all.'

'A nervy and edgy old Welsh fart,' Bo said, quietly, as the argument quietened.

The engineers and the electrician had quickly scoffed their entrees of Welsh rarebit on toast. Then the main courses they'd ordered arrived: thickly cut sirloin steaks, fried egg, chips, half roast tomato and whole sweet corn with spikes attached.

Rupert gulped at this extravagance, the indulgence that the MD. had alluded to at his employment interview.

Rupert caught their eyes and said to them quietly, 'I must tell you this, the company will not allow this extravagance to continue. The company, for *my* pains, has chosen me to sort out the feeding rate. The Managing Director told me, quite bluntly, that crew are overfed, must think they're on daddy's yacht.

'Traditionally, at sea, Sunday is the day for a steak, as you all might well know. It might come down to that on here. I'll do what I can. Lorry drivers have a free meal the cost included in the freight rate. I could suggest a thinner cut steak for them and find savings that way. Please don't blame me if steak-as-you-know-it isn't available every dinnertime.'

'Will it affect the crowd?' Bo asked, cutting off a sizeable chunk cooked rare.

'You're not telling me they have the choice, every day, too, are you?' Rupert asked, his eyes widening.

'I think they've always had a better chance of getting a daily steak than we have, but.' Bo said, 'their mates do the cooking and they're a militant crowd down below, but.'

'I see,' mumbled Rupert, his forehead creasing. He'd not found Asian crews bolshie whilst deep sea. 'I'll have to find out if the company will compromise on the indulgence, but I cannot see how, from what the MD instructed me.'

Two second mates entered the saloon and took another corner table. Rupert nodded towards them. Cara removed his empty soup bowl and took his order of roast beef. When the course arrived, he could see the cooks had roasted the silverside beef medium rare, the way he liked it.

When he finished his dinner he returned to the purser's office.

Alf was pouring over a newspaper crossword, obviously not overworked. 'No problems to report,' Alf said, 'we have ten lorry drivers onboard, all fed, watered and bedded down in driver's cabins for the crossing. A dozen foot passengers are either in the cafeteria or in the recliner space, trying to doze off. Little chance, they have. Passengers are already spewing, isn't it. Kicking up a bit too much for them, it is.

You've expenses claims to go through, though.' With that, he pushed a pile of forms towards him. 'Have fun,' he said, lurching with the roll of the ferry. He steadied himself and groped for the door.

'Hang on a minute, Alf,' Rupert said quickly. He'd spotted a woman approaching the hatch.

On a more northerly route, and at a different time of year, he thought she could be on her way to pick spuds: gather potatoes, Ayrshire earlies, on a coastal farm. A filthy and open donkey jacket hung over her broadish shoulders. She'd droopy breasts beneath a too-tight Guinness T-shirt, unkempt gingery hair, a face spotty with scratched sores, and a flattish nose. She'd tucked her Jeans into her wellies and her ten-pint-a-night Guinness belly was hanging over the length of rope she used as a belt.

He thought she'd also stink to high heavens. Truly, this was a pig with lipstick, a woman that might motivate Bo into action, if he could believe the tales of sexual daring to which he had proudly professed.

The woman opened her mouth and uttered words he didn't understand, thought they might be Irish Gaelic. He noticed, her chapped lips, and teeth broken and nicotine stained. He smartly stepped back a pace from the counter. Sighting the mischievously planted joke had turned his stomach earlier, a whiff of halitosis he didn't need now; he didn't want to speak to her at all!

'I need you to find this woman the person I believe she's looking for,' he told Alf. 'Nip into the saloon pantry and ask Cara to tell the second engineer that a girlfriend is asking for him at the office.'

Alf let out a chortle and swayed towards the door. 'You're catching on early to some of the Paddy jokers we have on here, isn't it, boss?'

Moments later, Bo's head poked around the corner of the saloon door. He took a quick look at the female asking after him. He wasn't impressed.

Quickly, Bo withdrew his head. Rupert was sure he heard him say, 'Screwfix, It's one of yours, but.'

Rupert hadn't noticed the ferry moving much as he sat in the saloon, but he detected a more alarming motion as he tried to keep his chair close to his desk. He was trying to understand the expenses claims and rule out what he found in the book titled Expenses Allowed and Disallowed. Satisfied with his assessments of crew claims, which, as far as he could tell were correct, unfiddled, he slipped the expense forms into an envelope to take to the head office in the morning.

It was a 4-hour crossing, normally; he knew that much. Because of the weather, he didn't have a clue what time the ferry would tie up in Holyhead harbour. He telephoned the bridge. The officer on watch told him not to expect arrival before midnight, but could be hours later, the ferry being on reduced speed. The availability of a berth was reliant on the ferries of other companies using the port able to keep to schedules. The Holigan Express might have to anchor outside and wait for a berth. The weather unlikely to improve anytime soon.

He checked his gabardine coat pocket and lifted out his mobile. He switched it on, wondering on the availability of a signal, the ferry being a mile or two from land already. Alas, no signal registered. Sophie would be out anyway, thinking up high-count scrabble words, but nothing as good or as valuable as the word 'yon'.

He glanced at the computer, then realised that it only connected with the internet in port.

He was mulling over what to do for the rest of the evening when a shadow fell over him through the hatch; the shadow was that of Dithery Dai.

'I'm Captain Dai Davis,' the captain said with a pronounced Welsh twang, 'Rupert, I'll meet with you at another time, but not tonight, though, I've got to get this hooligan of a vessel across our pond, but soon we'll get together, have a snifter. I keep Penderyn 12-year-old Welsh malt in my locker,' he said, with relish, his eyes twinkling. 'One of our great secrets is Penderyn Whisky. Nectar of our Welsh Gods isn't it. You Jocks don't have it all your own way in the whisky stakes. We can get to know one another when we compare. What do you say to that?' he asked.

'Your offer sounds good to me, Captain Davis. I like a dram now and again, preferably malt. Macallan is one of our finest distilleries. Their oak aged 12-year-old is one of Scotland's nicest and an affordable favourite of mine. It's so easy to drink, slides over the throat, stimulates the taste buds and lights up the eyes.'

The ferry lurched suddenly. Dithery Dai turned quickly, then walked awkwardly towards the door to the officer's accommodation and left the foyer.

Rupert pulled down and secured the shutters and locked up the office. It was in his mind to look for the officer's smoke room, which he thought would be in the officer's accommodation. He assumed that it was along the alleyway the captain had just entered. He wasn't interested in drinking anything, but curious about whom might be using it and what he might find in the smoke room and any entertainment it had to offer. The ferry looked too old to have TV beamed in by satellite. A dome he'd previously noticed above the bridge suggested the ferry did have the sophistication of satellite navigation.

The officers' smoke room was quite snug, decorated with all things Irish, their writers and their drinks all prominently displayed in poster form. Two faux leather settees sat at right angles along bulkheads. Card tables sat in front of the settees with chairs on the opposite side of them. A small bar dispensed Smithwicks dark beer on draught. No officers were using the smoke room to drink any. The keg beneath the bar could be empty. Didn't tell him crew could drink aboard. He saw dregs in the tray beneath the tap that told him they could. He switched on the television. All he saw was a whirling lines, no picture.

The ferry was lurching and jerking each time a wave hit it. The stabiliser fins were acting to reduce rolling but were unable to quell the pitching. Rupert thought a further tour of the cafeteria was too dangerous an undertaking, especially if passengers had stretched out; half of them were throwing up, Alf had said.

It was early to turn in, but he went into his bedroom and flopped onto the bunk. It was safer than trying to remain standing or sitting: the weather wasn't abating.

Rupert had fallen asleep, half dressed. He wakened about midnight, the ferry shuddering as it hit waves, which he could hear crashing over the ferry's bows and washing down the sides. He dressed for bed and slid beneath the duvet.

Chapter 5

HOLYHEAD Thursday Morning

When Rupert awoke next morning, the sounds of the ferry's bow lurching into deep troughs and howl of the wind were gone. The ferry was steady. He had slept through the high sea buffeting; as he had done on stormy nights during his deep-seagoing career. No daylight showed through gaps in his porthole curtains.

He reached behind his head and clicked on his reading light. His bedside alarm clock showed 7 a.m. The ferry moved on a light swell, squeezing a squeak from a rubber fender attached to the dockside. The sound confirmed to him that the Holigan Express was in port and berthed.

He slipped out of the bunk and drew back the curtains from the porthole. Outside and beneath him the glare of dockside lights illuminated lines of lorries, Tugmaster tow-trucks shunting trailers, cranes stacking containers, and dockers in Gortex waterproofs splashing through windswept puddles. This was his first sight of the busy port of Holyhead; now it was in full flow.

He shaved and showered, changed his shirt and underwear and put on his full uniform. He locked up and entered the saloon for breakfast. It was only 7:30. He was on his own. Engineers he guessed would be busy with the business of keeping the engines, generators and auxiliaries in good working order, or sleeping, having been up on watches during the trip across. Deck officers would be discharging freight or sleeping.

Cara was particularly attentive, her breast pushing against his ear and lingering; twice whilst serving him with a bowl of cornflakes he felt her hard nipple. It happened again when she placed a full breakfast in front of him, when she removed his empty plate and when she brought him coffee and milk in a jug. It had happened too many times. He was certain it was no accident.

He'd glanced quickly in her direction when she passed. Each time she was smiling. Each time he'd noted the cleavage between her great set of tits, a vale of loveliness that he thought had been daringly exposed. He concentrated on his breakfast but a whiff of her delicate perfume was hard not to notice.

Cara's attention had physically aroused him. He thought better of showing he'd noticed her allures. He wasn't sure he had. Could be dangerous! Shipping companies frowned upon officers consorting with crew, in any form; he'd no desire to breach that taboo. Knowing that didn't quell his interest in Cara.

The office wall clock said it was 9 a.m. when he slipped on his gabardine. Fitting his steaming bonnet securely onto his head, he pulled the peak down sharply. He'd one or two things to report to the MD. and take the expense forms to the office, which was across the vehicle park.

He wanted to arrive at the office block with the bonnet intact; not pursuing it across the dock, through puddles, for docker's entertainment or it to balloon high into the air, to disappear into the harbour waters, he never to see it again. The significant, gusting wind didn't look like abating anytime soon. He took the stairs down to the lower vehicle deck.

The company office was a hundred yards away from the ramp. Pushing through the office swing doors, he found the corridor bustling with activity. Drivers queuing at the front desk were booking in lorries for the next sailing. He heard chatter in different accents and languages.

The clerk at the desk, recognising he was an officer, said, helpfully, in a lilting accent he thought somewhere between Welsh and Scouse, 'The boss is in his office, if it's him you want.'

He made his way through a line of desks, knocked on the Managing Director's door and stood waiting a reply. The door opened and a woman with curly-blonde hair peeked from behind it, showing just a smile and her head.

'Rupert Sewell, purser on the Holigan Express, here to see the MD,' he said.

'Come in, Rupert, Fred will see you now,' the woman said in a husky voice. 'I'm Abi, his wife.'

'Ah, Rupert,' Fred said, from the far side of the oval table littered with paperwork and surrounded by chairs. A decanter holding a golden coloured liquid stood next to a half-full goblet, within easy reach of Fred's right hand. 'This is Abigail, my wife, though we all know her as Abi,' Fred said, 'She acts as my personal assistant and as personnel officer for the company, dealing with ferry officers and crew. Come and sit down and I'll get coffee brought in.

Rupert thought that Abi was about forty. A slender woman, she wore a body-hugging dress, showing her great chassis, which Rupert gave a quick once-over.

Abi hadn't missed his glance. She smiled back at him, without blushing, her eyes lingering on his, her lightly rouged lips parting seductively.

The office was stiflingly hot. Fred sat with his shirt sleeves rolled up, the shirt open at the neck. Rupert removed his steaming bonnet, knocked raindrops from it and hung it on the arm of a chair. His gabardine he hung over the back of a neighbouring chair. He then pulled out the chair facing the MD. from beneath the table and sat down. Abi pulled out the chair next to him and sat down; quite too close to him, he thought. As her knee pressed against his, he got a whiff of her delicate perfume, probably expensive and French.

'I've only had half a day on Holigan Express, but I've given thought to the catering on board,' he said. 'You were correct. I found items that need sorting out and I have ideas to put to you. Perhaps you already know of them, but I have a list in my head.'

'Good man, I hoped you would find methods to sort the elements that aren't as profitable as I'd like,' Fred said, looking up briefly from a document.

'Cameras above tills to record all transactions. The omission of cameras creates an opportunity for crew members to fiddle if that's what they're doing.'

Fred responded, 'We know they would help but haven't fitted them because it's an expensive installation. It's a chartered ferry, and I don't want to spend unnecessary money on it. And I'd need to have someone check the recordings.'

Fred was still messing with papers littering his desk. What Rupert said didn't seem of great interest to him.

'The opportunity to fiddle in the bar, the barman smuggling his own stock onboard to place on optic, is another cause for concern. Bar staff can easily fiddle the till in that operation.'

Rupert thought that should get Fred's attention.

'I didn't know about that. And you think that's what's going on?' Fred asked, raising his head from the papers, taking interest in his findings. He took a sip from the goblet and then looked towards Rupert.

'From my interview with you, you suspected it was,' Rupert replied, tensed. He had felt fingers land on his thigh, the one closest to Abi, then slowly stroking it.....all five fingers of a hand, the nails running over the barathea of his trousers, making him uneasy, wondering what was happening. He didn't flinch, but thought it placed him in an odd situation. Then he felt the fingers circle his thigh and squeeze it, three times, ever so gently.

Without a quiver in his voice he said, 'You were correct about sirloin steaks. It seems any crewmember can order one for dinner and on any day of the week. If you want to cut the feeding rate, I need instructions on that indulgence.'

The hand began to move between his thighs. He quickly snapped his legs closed. The hand remained in position, trapped. Then, with a sawing motion, the hand slowly forced its way towards his erection, a stronger one than he had earlier when Cara had served him breakfast. This erection had burgeoned quickly, straining to straighten to hardness in his boxers, getting ready to spring, to smack into Abi's hand, giving her the thrill that she was looking for, when he dared parting his thighs, leaving a gap, for Abi to explore further!

What should he do? He hadn't been in the job a day. If he let out a roar, pushed her chair away, toppling her to the floor showing his displeasure, he could see his job of purser on the Holigan Express ending quickly. If Fred knew, he either didn't give a shit or his brain had become so addled with alcohol that he didn't worry that his wife had nymphomaniac tendencies, had a fondness to sexually molest company workers, get them up, even when he was nearby and might notice.

His foreskin was stretching. Pressure against his boxers was pulling it back, paining him. Separating his thighs slightly to ease the discomfort, his erection found the fly opening in his boxers and sprang through, slapping into Abi's exploring hand. She gently squeezed the head of his penis, shuddered; then she slid her hand slowly away, dragging her nails across the barathea of his trousers, letting out an almost inaudible sigh, intended for only him to hear, he was sure.

Where was this going to lead, Rupert wondered. Irking was a moment or two away. He had to keep calm and did, didn't want to panic, give the game away. Was she after 'yon', was she after his body. Could he resist her advances. Did he want to?

He was home safe. If only for a millisecond. Abi was saying, 'I could do a round trip and assess Rupert's assertions.'

'Of course, you could sort out the problems here in this office,' Rupert hastily responded; speaking quickly because he felt he had to. He didn't want to appear keen to entertain the MD's wife on board, in his bunk, assertions turning into insertions! 'I mean, you could become a cashless ferry, insist on the use of credit and debit cards on board, place an extra charge on tickets to cover a meal. You could also have in place machines vending sandwiches, as well as tea, coffee, and soft drinks. That would tighten control considerably; take cash out of crew hands, reduce crew levels, even.'

Fred replied, looking directly at Rupert, 'Cruise companies work the card system. I would have to investigate how it might work in practice on Holigan Express. When you go back onboard, have the steward make the owner's suite fresh and presentable. Abi will want to relax in the comfort it affords. When she is through with her inspection, she'll want to write up her report in private.'

The coffee arrived. Rupert couldn't stand up; he just opened his jacket, picked up the coffee pot and got ready to pour.

*

As soon as Rupert was out the door, Fred put his pen down. Sliding the paperwork he was working on to one side he dribbled golden liquid into the goblet. Topped up, he took a sip, rolled the sip around his mouth, swallowed, then said to Abi, 'Well, what are your thoughts on our new purser. Do you think he can suss out our losses onboard? Do you think he can resist the temptations of the female flesh that the ferry has in large, and dangerous, it seems, proportions?'

Abi hadn't moved from her chair seated opposite Fred. She had waited for him say something. She answered, 'Rupert was at sea on ships that had female passengers onboard for months, much longer than a ferry crossing. He could have dallied with those interested or tempted into a seaboard romp. I don't know if he is sexually inclined that way,' she lied, having had first-hand experience, enjoyable and as encouraging as it was, of his arousal.

'We will have to see,' Abi continued, 'the autopsy report on Hugh that we received yesterday didn't confirm the rumour that the manner of his death was a sexual partner on top and underneath or on each side of him. It could be that he was having sex with one or both of the stewardesses and suffered a heart attack, though we've no positive proof that that happened. No other female passengers travelled that crossing. He had died before the ambulance took him to hospital. I doubt the rest of the crew know of all the circumstances. A sandwich between those to lumps of flesh, unable to breath. And Hugh was only a slight person, not an ounce of spare flesh; skin and bone, built like a whippet, he was. Poor man. I hope he died happy.'

Fred asked, 'Do you think we should warn Rupert of the dangers of fraternising with the stewardesses?'

'He's only had a single crossing. No. What would he think of our company if we were to warn him, explain the dangers of fraternising with the female crewmembers? He might walk down the gangway again and where would we be. No. If he does the job we need from him, he will cast a different impression to Hugh. He was a bit soft. He was lashing out too much overtime to Cara and Tara. The sandwich could have been the way they extracted it. Screwing him might've been his reward. What a way to go, huh?'

*

Rupert walked a little stiffly back towards the Holigan Express, his erection lingering. He tried to dump the encounter with Abi from his mind. He looked around, saw no dock personnel close by, opened his coat and jacket buttons, slid a hand down the inside of his trousers and made himself comfortable. He couldn't stop his mind reliving the feeling Abi's hand had given him. It was a thrill he didn't expect. Abi was going to board the ferry later that morning and hang around him all day, close to him, as they investigated the points he'd raised with Fred. Her resting up in the owner's suite scared him: would she invite him in. For sex! If her interest in his body continued, she'd swan onboard looking for sex from him, anywhere!

The prospect alarmed him! He wanted to keep this job. Would crew use threats if they found out. Could he remain safe from her predatory clutches. Could he stay out of the reach of her exploring hands. Could he refuse the offer he was sure she would make of a lunchtime aperitif in her cabin?

It was all a bit of a worry and he still had the envelope with the expense claims in his pocket.

Chapter 6

Rupert walked across the length of vehicle park, reaching the loading ramp, keeping an eye on the freight movements. Tugmaster tow trucks shunted loaded trailers into place at the bow end of the bottom deck. Lorries were parked in lines waiting for the unaccompanied freight to load. First off the ferry in the Irish port driver-accompanied lorries would be last to load in Holyhead.

On his way across the lorry-park and as he boarded the ferry, he'd been continually reliving Abi's touching-him-up in the MD's office, but not for more arousal. He'd found the sexual assault disturbing, more sexually threatening than the Cara incidents earlier that morning, in the saloon, at breakfast. He didn't want to put a foot wrong as he crossed the vehicle deck, either.

He took the designated footpath across the deck, concentrated on the activities going on around him; it was his first experience of a ferry loading freight. He noted dockers tightening the shackles that secured lorries and trailers loaded with all manner of stuff to the deck and watched the manoeuvrability of the Tugmasters positioning the loaded trailers, without wasting space.

In a flash of white, Bo Boyle, wearing his ultra-clean boilersuit and a pair of unstained working gloves, stepped out from behind a stationary Tugmaster, ending Rupert's thought train. 'Ru Ru Rupert,' he shouted above the noise of revving engines, stepping in close, to speak into Rupert's ear, 'thought I'd better warn you, a delegation from the crowd is waiting outside your office to speak to you. It seems a bollox has spread word that you're taking steaks from their daily menu choices, but. Normally, they're just looking for more coin in the pay packet, but this is different, affects their guts, not their pockets, but.'

'It's a company decision, not mine,' Rupert replied. He noticed that Bo grinned as he spoke: slyly, as if he would enjoy any grief heading his way. It crossed Rupert's mind that Bo might be that bollox, thought he'd hung about purposely to give him the news. He still hadn't worked out why Irish people ended their sentences with the word but. 'The MD's wife is boarding later. She's also the personnel officer. She'll deal with the complaint. She'll make the bullets; the cooks and I will have to fire them.'

'Ah, the lovely Abi,' Bo said, his eyes lighting up. 'I would certainly give her a length of the old knob, sure I would. She's no stumper, her, but. Tread carefully with the seamen's rep, Dick Drake. Your man's a right sea lawyer, he is to be sure, but. You will know him when you see the pair, but. Drake has a face like a pair o' kneed bollocks, all purplish, swollen, lopsided and hairy with a permanent pained expression, but. And his sidekick, Ted Higson, has a face like a mended kelt with warts. That pair certainly try to stir things up on here, but mainly Drake with Higson his supporting act.'

Rupert gulped at Bo's descriptions. He wasn't looking forward to the encounter with such persons. He would have Abi deal with their grievances when she came onboard. That could remove from her mind any idea of having sex with him.

As Rupert left the staircase from the vehicle deck and entered the foyer, he spotted two men leaning against the office grill. From Bo's descriptions, these were the seamen's reps. He was about to escape towards a door leading to the officers' accommodation when he heard the cry of 'Boss,' which most pursers responded to, when uttered by crew to gain their attention. He turned, approached the men, and asked, 'What can I do for you?'

'We'd like to speak to you about the no steaks for us crew as a daily menu choice decision,' said Dick Drake, in what Rupert thought was a Scouse accent. His facial features were as ghastly as Bo had described.

Dick Drake was thickset of body, about five feet, six inches tall, had a short neck, wore jeans, a paint-splattered lumberjack-style shirt open at the neck and showing a thick tuft of black hair. A bit of a bruiser who could handle himself and worked on deck, Rupert thought. Ted Higson dressed similarly. Both wore open donkey jackets.

He wasn't too sure of the sidekick's, mended kelt features. He would have to look up that description. He saw that Ted had a weak chin, his lips moving and silently repeating Dick Drake's words, as if he were in total agreement.

'Can you leave it for now,' Rupert said, 'the company personnel officer is sailing next trip. I'll get her to deal with it. Any change to feeding is the company's decision, not mine. You can negotiate with her; see how you get on. I must tell you that the managing director thinks steak as a daily menu choice is an extravagance. It's unlikely the personnel officer will disagree. As far as I can tell, the feeding rate is higher than Board of Trade requirements and you have little to gripe about.'

Glad to have dealt with the complaint, Rupert pirouetted on one foot and turned away. He heard Dick Drake let out a gasp and stamp a foot. He didn't see Drake or Higson pull faces as he walked away, or hear the whispered words, 'Another fucking arsehole.'

Rupert strode purposefully towards the door leading to the officer's accommodation. He thought he had better find Cara. Breakfast would be over and she should be making up officer's cabins. He wanted to tell her to make sure the owner's suite was ready for occupation.

*

'My cabin now,' Dick Drake said over his shoulder to Ted as he walked towards the staircase down to their cabins, Ted scurrying meekly behind him. In the cabin, the door locked from the inside, Dick said, 'This is how we play this. We must put on a show for the lads. We must keep a supply of steaks coming onboard, otherwise we'll have less to take with us on trip off.

'If we can get the company to agree to steak as a daily menu choice, more steaks will come onboard. And you know the number of nicked sirloins, cooked or raw, wrapped in plastic bags then secured around waists by gaffer tape we take with us on trip off day.

'We'll make a complaint and say to the new purser that the company are serving up horsemeat instead of beef. The Micks like to take a steak or two home as well. They might not be as militant as the Brits employed on here but thieving and what else they do to enhance their living standards are the same as ours. They might support us, but I wouldn't put money on it.'

'Tis true,' Ted volunteered, 'it's a good idea strapping the steaks to our guts, in case we get a bag search going trip off. My kids only taste sirloins when I go trip off, normally have to chew through a bit of tough rump off a cow's backside.'

'Mine too,' Dick said, 'I want to screw as much as I can from this ferry company. Other ferry companies are starting to use foreign crews on their ships. All the lads will be out of a job because of cheap labour from the Philippines and Thailand. We should grab what we can while we can.

'I expect Flick will have something to say about the stew turning into curry overnight. I wouldn't be a bit surprised if he mentions it to that prick Rrrrrupert,' Dick said, 'I expect the cooks will lockdown the skylight, and seal off our unofficial galley entry and exit, if he reports it. We might have to put the hard word on Flick to ease off.

'If Flick is unwilling to continue ignoring our nicking, then we might have to issue a threat or two. He won't want to lose this number as he's local. He can go home every day for an hour while we're in port. The job suits him. He couldn't get one better. He'll get his end away each time he goes home. That's the luck of the Micks, to be sure.

'The girls sorted out Hugh Rice ok, though nobody saw his end coming that way, when *he* was getting his end away. What a way to go. One can only dream.'

Chapter 7

Rupert stepped through the doorway to the officer's accommodation, let the door swing closed and then stopped. He mused: he hadn't been aboard the ferry twenty-four hours, yet he seemed embroiled in various awkward scenarios. None were of his own making if he could discount getting a steaming erection as Abi touched him up, under the table, in her husband's office, her feeling its presence, as his erection launched like a homing projectile to strike her eagerly exploring hand.

It wasn't the place to clear his head, he was sure, so he walked on, past the officer's bar, to the adjacent cabins. The electrician's cabin door was open as he passed. Screwfix, which was the only name he had for the electrician, was stripping down a vacuum cleaner, bits littering his deck, ready to fit it with a new cable.

He took a step back and knocked on the cabin door. Screwfix smiled a welcome and said, 'Don't just look in, come on in.' Rupert heard the broad Irish accent, that he thought was from the Republic; certainly, his speech was a softer brogue than that of Bo Boyle.

'I'm looking for Cara,' he said, surveying the cabin, tidy apart from the bits lying on the deck. 'I was sure she should be making cabins up along here. He saw that Cara had already neatly made up the bunk, placing folded pyjamas atop the pillows.

A choice of screwdrivers, other tools and test meters littered the electrician's desk.

'To be sure, she's been and gone down here. She'll be upstairs doing the deck officer's cabins by now,' Screwfix said.

'I haven't had much time to look around yet,' Rupert replied. 'I suppose I'll find out where I'm going in time.'

'You'll have passed a staircase up to the next deck as you came by the officer's bar door. It takes you to the mates' cabins, the captain's, the chief engineer's, and the owner's suite. You'll find a staircase up to the bridge on that deck as well.'

'Ah, good,' Rupert said, 'I wondered where the owner's cabin might be. The MD's wife is travelling this afternoon and will be using it. I'd better make sure it's ready.'

'Ah, the lovely Abi,' Screwfix said, parroting Bo's words but omitting the words giving her a length of the old knob.

Rupert thought the Irish personnel he'd met since joining the ferry certainly had rare turns of phrase. Then he asked, 'You're not provided with a workshop on here. You have to work from your cabin?'

The workshop is a lock-up on the top freight deck. It's too bloody cold to be spending time in it at this time of year, but,' Screwfix replied.

'You must have a proper name, too, Screwfix being a nickname, surely?' Rupert chided.

I was baptised Patrick O'Donohue, but I don't mind what I get,' Screwfix said. 'Bo has chosen different handles for officers on here, even if it doesn't fit the character, to be sure. Normally on ships the chief engineer is The Corned beef. Roger Staines, our Chief Officer, has a lady friend he visits in Holyhead on the lay-over on weekends and returns to the ferry looking shagged out. He doesn't know yet but he is known onboard as Comestaines. Amongst the names the rest of us call Bo is El Sobriquet, but nobody has told him yet, but. He'll have one for you before too long, you wait and see. We're just seagoing acquaintances on here, as on any merchant ship. Onboard nicknames don't follow you home, either.'

'I must admit, I know little about ferrying, or the history of this boat,' Rupert said, hoping to hear an account from Patrick.

'This ferry is a charter job,' Patrick said, 'the company flew a crew out to Greece to pick her up. The entire personnel on here worked on a ferry sailing out of Fishguard to Dun Laoghaire, but the company went tits up a year ago.

'I'm sure we were all glad when this job turned up. We get good wages and time off, to be sure. The company is intent on building Ballymagilligan into a larger port with a reliable ferry service. If they do that, and if trade keeps on picking up, like it's doing, then we'll get steady employment.'

'I'll learn a little every day, for a while,' Rupert admitted, 'so I'll move on and look upstairs.'

Rupert found the short staircase and climbed up a deck. He found himself standing in an alleyway the bulkheads painted the customary creamy colour, but not recently. Looking both ways, he saw a door to a deck at one end, at the other a cross alleyway. He walked towards the cross alleyway. He knew that senior officer's cabins would have the prime locations with portholes facing forward.

The captain and the chief engineer had those cabins. The chief officer and the owner's suite had doors on the cross alleyway, but had side cabins, with no forward-facing portholes. A door at each end of the alleyway led onto an open deck. Both the chief engineer and the captain had closed their cabin doors. He assumed that they were catching up on lost sleep, having been up early taking the ferry into port.

A black, plastic rubbish bag lay outside the chief officer's cabin. He walked towards it. A vacuum bursting into life in the cabin; that and the bag outside suggested that Cara was working in the cabin.

Rupert reached the door and looked in. A view of Cara bending over to move a pair of shoes out of the way of her vacuum nozzle confronted him. His first thought was that her bottom looked firm, wondrous, cuddly, and tightly packed into her black trousers. Cara straightened and looked behind her. 'No you don't, Boss,' she said, giving him the wickedest of smiles. 'What can I do for you?' she asked, switched the appliance off and turned to face him.

Slightly taken aback by her reply, he looked away, feigning shyness, and asked, 'The owner's suite. Do you have a key?'

'To be sure,' she said, taking a bunch of keys from a pocket, 'I have a pass key for all the cabins up here and down below.'

'Let's have a look then. The MD's wife is travelling next trip,' he said and began to walk away.

Chapter 8

Back in his office, the crew expense claims out of a pocket and on the desk, his raincoat and steaming bonnet hung up behind the door, Rupert glanced at his wristwatch as he pulled down his jacket sleeve. It was 11 a.m. He wondered where the morning had gone. He had no idea when the ferry would sail again so he picked up the office phone and dialled the navigation bridge number. A seaman cleaning salt from the outside of the bridge windows answered his call. He didn't know; no deck officer was on the bridge to ask.

Rupert looked out the porthole and noted lorries were lining up ready to reverse towards the ramp then down it onto the deck. Dockers working the deck would guide them into position for the crossing, then shackle them down so they couldn't move. Abi would be leaving the office block soon. Striding across the trailer park she'd have to dodge around puddles as she progressed. Thinking he'd keep out of her way, he then picked up the PA microphone and made an announcement for the second steward to report to the office.

When Alf appeared, Rupert asked, 'What is going on? Have you heard when we're sailing?'

'It should be any time soon,' Alf said, 'but we're not going to get back on schedule. We rarely do. When bad weather increases passage times we usually only get back on schedule on Mondays, after the lay over in Holyhead.'

'Okay. When do we open the office for enquiries, etcetera?'

'We should have been open by now. Lorry drivers in cabins are already getting their heads down.'

Rupert thought quickly. 'I want you to open up whilst I have a check round. I must get a feel for the job. If you need me, just make the announcement. I won't be far away.'

The office grill opened, and Alf seated, Rupert dashed towards the staircase taking him down to the galley. He was sure he could lose himself further down in the storerooms, and stay out of Abi's clutches, if only for a while, for he knew he had to meet with her.

Passing through the cafeteria on his escape route from a meeting with Abi, a female voice shouting Boss stopped him in his tracks. He looked towards the voice. It was coming from behind the cafeteria servery. Just visible above the counter, he saw a round-faced woman with long, flowing black hair and a twinkle in her eyes.

She looked a good bit shorter than Cara did. Whilst he was walking towards the servery, the woman stood up from the stool she'd been sitting on, revealing her true height. She was immense, broad of shoulder and towering over the counter and him. She wore stewardesses' uniform. Beneath the open top, he could see she was revealing the cleavage between the largest pair of tits he had ever ogled.

Was she from County Waxford, shot into his mind? Silly me, he thought, knowing it was County Wexford he should have been thinking of instead of tit sizes. He tried to work out if Wexford was a mountainous County, had anything pointing skywards like County Kerry's Macgillycuddy Reeks.

'I'm Tara,' she said.

He noticed Tara's tits were straining any device she was wearing to hold them in position, with nipples to poke out your eyes. He just couldn't take his eyes from the enticing, fleshy valley between them.

Tara noticed. 'No you don't, boss,' she said. He noted she used the same words that Cara had said to him, in the same lilting, Irish accent and was sporting the same wicked smile.

Rupert quickly composed himself and looked away, whilst saying, ' I'll get to know all of the crew eventually, but it will take time.'

'I'm Cara's older sister,' she said, 'by just a year or two. She's officers' steward, serves you in the saloon and does your cabin.'

Just then, voices announced the arrival of passengers or lorry drivers into the cafeteria. He used that as an excuse to leave and said, 'Well Tara, I'm sure I'll bump into you again. I'll leave you now. You could be busy,' Rupert said, then turned and said 'Hello,' to two drivers as they entered the cafeteria. He strode off towards the galley.

It flashed through Rupert's mind as he walked away how he might look atop any of the two buxom beauties, Tara and Cara, with Abi wrestling them to get at his body. He walked quickly on, hoping that the vision hadn't triggered any visible arousal.

In the galley, the chief cook, his new assistant, Hamish MacNab, and the galley boy were in a huddle, having a chat, waiting for passenger orders. Hamish had gravy stains down his cook's attire and a towel hanging from a shoulder. He smiled, looked happy to be back at sea.

Steaks were smoking beneath a grill. On separate trays pork chops, bacon and sausages lay, partially cooked for heating through later, when orders came in: a cook's short cut to faster food for fried meat that Rupert knew of. Steam rose from deep fryers as chips blanched. On the range, a pot of potatoes, one of carrots, another of peas and a small pot of baked beans all simmered alongside a larger pan of soup. The scene wasn't new to him.

His nostrils detected the powerful smell of curry. He knew that Friday was the traditional day for curry aboard white crewed merchant ships. Why it was bubbling away on the range today, he wondered. Flick Fleck saw him investigate the pot contents and guessed why. He approached Rupert and said, 'It's for lunch today. A day earlier than usual, to be sure.'

'Why the change?' Rupert asked.

'Last night, when I locked up the galley, it was a pot of beef and vegetable stew. When I opened the galley this morning, it had turned, miraculously, into curried beef and veg and half of it was missing.'

He looked directly at Rupert, a serious look on his face. Then he cast his eyes upwards towards the galley skylight. Then he pointed to the metal ladder secured to the bulkhead leading up to the deckhead. 'We have hungry pigs seafaring on here. Don't think they're well-enough fed. I could name culprits capable of getting in through the skylight to steal food.'

'They hungered after a midnight feast?' Rupert asked, shaking his head. 'It's not as if they're underfed on here, as far as I can tell.'

'That's about right, but. Crew eat well and it's all good produce we use. We could lock the skylights at night when we're not cooking, I suppose, maybe have extra metal bars welded across the skylight so that greedy bastards cannot get through. But I reckon that would be a refit or a job when we go to drydock. I don't fancy weld splatter contaminating food prepared by any of us. And who wants to climb up the ladder, hang on with one hand whilst they fit the locks each night, I ask you? You won't get me going up a height, that's for sure. Especially in rough weather.' Flick said, looking directly at Rupert.

'I'll mention the problem to management. The MD.'s wife travels today, and I'll broach the subject along with complaints about the removal of steaks from the crew menu. What's your opinion on that issue?' Rupert asked the cook.

'A steak is easier cooked. A dash of salt and pinch of pepper, minutes on the hotplate and it's ready to flash off later under the grill, for sure, but. Fries and salads are on the cafeteria menu. The items on the crew and officer's menu adds to the considerable workload for two cooks and a galley boy. The pressure can go on until late at night sometimes. We do get overtime, of course.'

As Rupert was turning to leave, Dick Drake walked into the galley with Ted Higson a pace behind. 'Ah, boss, Dick said, looking up towards the skylight, his eyes averting Rupert's, 'I'm glad we bumped into you here.' Glaring directly into Rupert's face now, looking for a reaction, he said loudly, 'Our complaint now is that the company is supplying horsemeat to replace beef on crew menus. Ted and I are of the opinion that the meat served up as beef on here doesn't taste right. That's why we want a steak choice twice daily and it must be a beef sirloin. It's either that or we inform health inspectors, both here in Holyhead and in the Republic of our concerns.

'They will cause trouble and bad publicity, even if they find nothing. Be it on your head if you attract that attention for the company.'

Rupert noticed that the second cook had moved closer and was listening intently to the conversation. The chief cook, his back turned, was shaking his head.

The suggestion rocked Rupert. He shook his head in disbelief, pirouetted on one foot, and let out a gasp. What had he dived into by taking this job was to the forefront of his mind? Everywhere he looked or parked his backside he was finding irksome problems. Perhaps, because of this new complaint, he should not delay his meeting with Abi, let her sort out the problems, even if this one sounded ridiculous, nasty, false and a load of horseshit.

He walked quickly past the agitators. Shaking his head in disbelief, ignoring them, he was telling them he wasn't interested, their complaint had no validity. But to make sure nothing resembling horsemeat was lurking in the fridges, he took the stairs down to the storeroom flat situated beneath the main vehicle deck.

Empty cardboard boxes littered the flat floor. He'd instruct someone to get it cleared up and put into a rubbish skip. The outer door padlock to the cold rooms was hanging open on the eye. He removed it, placed it in a coat side pocket, folded back the hasp and pulled the door open.

He stepped into the preparation and defrosting area. The light switch was outside the door. He put the light on and pulled the door closed behind him. The clock style gauge outside the meat room door showed that the room was down to temperature as were the dairy and vegetable rooms.

Inside the meat room he inspected boxes, not piled as high as they would be on deep-sea ships. Stores were deliverable daily or when needed to the Holigan Express, not every few weeks until the ship reached the next port on the voyage. The packages, both open and closed, he examined.

Although he had no knowledge of how different horsemeat cuts might look, he pictured an equine sirloin steak to be of greater dimensions than that carved from a bullock. From the labels and the meat cut sizes, he was sure nothing of that ilk lurked in the fridges now: nothing that said succulent slices of Clydesdale rump, Irish Cob silverside, thoroughbred horse fillet or tongue and sweetbreads of donkey. He would need to find a way to be sure, to be sure. He let out a titter at his unintentional Irishism.

Then it came to him: why didn't the ferry company shop ashore, at supermarkets and market gardens for supplies. His experience of ship's chandlers supplying foodstuffs, in any port in the world where he had placed an order, usually resulted in chandlers presenting an inflated price list, these providers having a monopoly on the ship supply business.

Pursers always expected a backhander, the baksheesh, of course, and that could be quite considerable when storing for a long voyage. Rupert was sure that crew on every ship suspected the existence of the bribe to pursers. Pursers never admitted to it, of course. He did know that pursers ordered inferior cuts of Mohammedan killed mutton rather than lamb from Indian chandlers, receiving an enhanced baksheesh. He doubted a ferry purser received a backhander in a brown envelope from shoreside suppliers. The head office was too close to the port. Clerks ashore would order the ferry victualing requirements.

As he closed the meat room door, he heard a rattling from outside the outer door. It didn't concern him, but when he pushed on the door to get out, it didn't move and swing open. He tried again, this time with a more robust heave, jarring his shoulder in the process. He looked around for an alarm push. Then the lights went out.

He had noted the position of the mushroom-shaped plunger of an alarm when he looked around the defrost area. In the dark, he followed the bulkhead until he felt the box with the alarm push. With his palm over the push, he was hoping that Screwfix the electrician was up to his job and all alarms were working.

No sound rang out other than the clang of metal on metal as the push moved. He thought the alarm should sound in the galley, the cook sending the galley boy down to see what the problem was. He would just have to wait and see.

He had a go at guessing why the imprisonment had happened. In his mind, Dick Drake and his cohort were the chief suspects. Boaby, the prick, run them a close second. It was either another silly Boaby prank or Dick Drake and Ted Higson delivering a threatening message, they proving to the crew that they had worthy representation. If that was the case, Rupert was beginning to believe they were acting irresponsibly. Boaby was well spotted, but clearly other pricks worked onboard the ferry.

Chapter 9

Abi had boarded Holigan Express quite often. She knew her way around the decks and walked purposefully, a hand swinging an overnight bag, in the other a handbag and briefcase, down the loading ramp, then onto the lower vehicle deck. She took her time following the designated route across the deck, looking to see that dockers were not wasting space when they parked a lorry and shackled it down. Dockers looked towards her leeringly, Tugmaster drivers tooted. She smiled; the only clue that she'd reacted to their attention. Loading was going ahead. The waiting freight would fill the ferry on the return voyage.

Inside the central housing, she stood to one side of the staircase as she recognised the galley boy on his way down. 'You're in a rush, Tommy,' she said casually to him. She took pride in knowing crewmember first names but not all of them.

'The cold room alarm's just gone off. I'm on my way to see what's up, missis.' Tommy had no other word for addressing her.

'I'll come down with you,' she replied, 'that's one place on the ship I haven't been.'

Rupert heard a metallic sound. Was someone pulling the outer door handle. Relief, he heard the click of the bolt moving. The lights came back on. The door opened. He was surprised to see Abi standing looking in, her face breaking into a smile of recognition, the smile quite as alluring as it was earlier that morning.

Tommy the galley boy was holding a welding rod, bent like a hairgrip. 'This was keeping the lever from moving and the door shut,' he blurted out.

'Well, well Rupert, what do we call this?' Abi asked.

'It looks like a silly prank of some sort,' Rupert replied, trying to keep his cool.

'It also looks like we have things of importance to discuss. Let's adjourn to your office,' Abi said, throwing her head slightly towards the stairs. 'Tommy can lock up here.'

He handed Tommy the padlock from his pocket and to show he had noticed the empty boxes littering the stores flat, he said to him, 'Tell the chief cook I'd like this mess shifted and dumped ashore, as soon as possible.' He then followed Abi up the stairs. He couldn't draw his eyes away from her fine pair of legs. Her dress was knee length, showing her calves; the right calf he noticed was slightly thinner than the left one. It occurred to him that he shouldn't have been looking at them at all, and earlier that morning he shouldn't have been looking at Cara's behind, thinking it cuddly or at her sister Tara's great tits and allowing his eyes to linger over the magnificent, fleshy, enticing valley between them. Ferry Life!

Chapter 10

Reaching the top of the staircase, Abi turned into the alleyway leading to the galley. She developed a longer stride. Tommy had locked the cold rooms quickly and raced past Rupert on the stairs. He couldn't match Abi's longer stride. The pair of loose fitting, gravy-and-oil-stained leather boots with no laces were holding him back.

Rupert eased past Tommy, taking up a position a yard behind Abi. He got a whiff of her interesting perfume as he followed her through the galley entrance.

Both cooks left what they were doing on seeing her. Rubbing their hands with towels, they approached the range, keeping it and the steaming pots between them and Abi.

'Whatever you've in the pot for lunch sure smells good,' Abi said, looking across the range.'

'A tasty beef and veg Madras curry,' the chief cook responded, 'better than you will get ashore, for sure, plus the trimmings.' He omitted explaining the surprise nature of the meal.

'I take it you're getting all the stores that you order,' she asked.

'Everything we ask for,' chief cook said, though I've had to listen to grumbles from the crew rep.'

'I see,' Abi responded, as her eyes scanned other parts of the galley.

Before Abi could ask for any details, Rupert butted in. 'I've a crew feeding problem to discuss with you. Better sort it in my office, I think.'

'I'll see you again before I go off tomorrow if anything else is bothering you, tell me then,' she said to the chief cook, 'I'll enjoy your curry at lunch.' Then she turned, grabbed Rupert by the arm, squeezed it and pulled him towards the galley door. The arm squeeze enough for Rupert's mind to raise an unwanted presence in his boxers and it start looking for the escape route it found earlier that morning.

Rupert pushed open the office door and allowed Abi to enter first. 'You can go now', he said to Alf, 'I have business to discuss with the personnel officer. Alf rose from the chair, closed the paper he was reading, folded it, stuffed it in a side pocket and left without a word.

Rupert moved the chair Alf was sitting on to one side of the desk, for his use. He carried the chair from his bedroom for Abi to use, positioning it in front of the desk, giving it a quick dusting with the palm of one hand then ensuring a decent space existed between it and the one on which he would sit.

Abi didn't move her chair closer to his and he was pleased about that. The grill was up. Anyone in the foyer would glimpse any shenanigans going on. He hadn't tucked his legs under a great, concealing table, but a narrow desk. He could safely get down to official business.

'Ok. What problem do you want to talk about?' Abi asked, looking at him and smiling.

'It's unbelievable, Rupert said, tapping the desk with a finger, 'the crew rep has alleged we've been serving up horse meat to the crowd. That's why I went to the cold rooms to check. Of course, I found nothing I could identify as horse in the meat room or in the others.

'It appears they're disappointed that steak will not be a menu choice for them every day as per the MD's, instructions to me. I had only mentioned the directive to the engineers at dinner last night. It seems news has quickly spread to the crowd.'

'Monstrous,' Abi erupted, 'they're overfed as it is. Horse meat! Huh! Take no shit from them, Rupert. Always refer them to feeding rates with other companies. On here, crew and officers' feeding is superior, well above what other companies offer and of Board of Trade requirements.

'We cannot account for the number of steaks consumed on here. The company isn't showing a profit in the services and the cafeteria till hasn't the sophistication to record individual sale types. We are attending to that. A new till is on order. It will list individual menu items from cups of tea to steaks. We should get a better idea where the steaks are going. It will even tally teabag and coffee pod use. We can update it to show menu changes, though none of the choices will be fancy, just cafeteria fare, we've no restaurant as such.

'Now do you have anything else?' she asked, 'It's customary that I see the captain when I come on board. I should do that now. I will see you later for a tour of all other areas and look at the concerns you have highlighted. Then together we will meet the crew rep and listen to his bolshie rants.'

Rupert wasn't going to tell Abi that unknown cooks had doctored the curry she was keen to sample at lunch. He hoped that the chief cook had ensured the curry safe and edible.

He had to mention the galley security issue to ensure food theft never happened again. He said, 'Evidence exists that crew members are guilty of galley theft at night, when it's closed, by lifting the skylight, and descending the ladder and helping themselves to anything on the stove. The cooks open and close the skylight with the long pole, but anyone can lift the skylight from the deck above.

'I'm sure ship's engineers can make up a length of wire rope to secure the skylight to a lower rung of the ladder. The cooks can secure it handily with a padlock and release it when necessary. I'll have a word with the chief engineer to see if they can mock something up. If not, I'll have them make a drawing for you to order ashore if that's ok with you. Anything more permanent and secure we can organise at a refit.'

'Who knows what has gone missing. I'll speak to the chief engineer. Let me know how it goes,' Abi said, then opened her briefcase, took out the ship's articles and said, 'Sign on in the first vacant space and phone the galley. Get the second cook to do the same.'

Rupert handed over the expense claims to Abi, explaining his earlier oversight.

Abi said, 'Thank you. I'll deal with them. It's usual that I eat with the captain at his table when I'm onboard. Can you tell the stewardess to lay a place for me?'

Chapter 11
Log 1 of Hamish MacNab

About 14:00 on Wednesday 4th January, I stepped out of a taxi onto Ballymagilligan Harbour. It was cold, the blustery gale-force wind making it chillier. I could see no places to shelter, no Gardai or Custom posts and only minimal office buildings. I thought the harbour deserted, apart from lines of cars and lorries. I saw a man standing alone, close to a vehicle ramp. He was wearing a bonnet favoured by the officer classes and thought him waiting to join the ferry. I walked over to him and introduced myself. He was Rupert Sewell, the purser, and would be my boss onboard. We had a short chat of little significance.

A ferry had negotiated the inlet and neared the only available berth. I saw people dressed differently to the purser walking onto the harbour. They looked more like lower deck crew. I left the purser to join them.

Introductions confirmed the others were a mixed bunch of deck, engine room and catering personnel, rejoining the ferry following a trip off. Their names will take me time to remember. From their accents, all were Irish. The two big lumps of women that Commander Dewsnap had described were amongst them. I noticed both of them eyeing me up and down, nudging each other; I must have looked attractive to them, I was sure. I showed no concern, no overt interest that either woman attracted me. I only glanced briefly in the women's general direction and smiled.

I heard bottles rattling together in a holdall as a crewmember repositioned it on the ground. I learned from banter that he was the barman. I asked if the crowd had a Pig. A crewmember told me they did have a crew bar and recreation area, but it only served a weak beer, on draught.

It became clear from the expletive strewn conversations of the rejoining personnel that the ferry wasn't going to berth in the adverse weather conditions. The general opinion crewmembers mouthed accused the captain of being dithery, who had, during an earlier storm, failed in his attempt to dock the ferry when a gale blew and the tide was ebbing.

Crewmembers made loud utterances damning the captain but weren't too displeased. I followed the crowd to Gilligan's, the pub situated on Harbour Road, to wait a successful docking. I took it from banter I heard that certain crewmembers were returning to their earlier, pre-boarding meeting place of that afternoon.

The Bar of the pub had basic furnishings: padded but worn wall seating, wooden tables, plastic chairs, and bar stools with padding thin and uncomfortable enough to numb one's arse if one sat on one too long.

A jukebox was playing a Sawdoctor's tune as I entered. Keltic rock numbers the crowd's musical choices throughout my stay. Finbar Fury, Fergal Sharkey, Gary Moore and Thin Lizzy the popular listening. I noted that excellent Scottish, should-have-made-it, rock band of the nineteen-seventies, and later, Iron Claw, had tracks played. The puggy had a pile of Euro coins shoved into it with little reward for the gambler.

I bought a pint of Guinness from the barman. I suspected he was Eastern European. I thought, from his swarthy, facial features, Romanian.

The inflated cost in Euros of a pint of the stout, just up the road from the Dublin brewery, compared to the cheaper prices normal in the pubs of distant Glasgow, was scandalous, astonished me. Two of the crowd were in deep conversation with the barman. I was never close enough to hear a word said. From where I was sitting, I could see the entire bar area. The only customers were the crew who had walked from the dock with me. Including the two stewardesses, we were eighteen in total.

I sat with my back to a wall in the seated area alongside crewmembers. It didn't take long before one asked me my credentials.

I explained that I was joining the ferry as a relief and didn't expect a full-time job, though I would be interested if one became available. I also explained that, in the past, I had cooked at sea, that I had gone ashore and been self-employed delivering produce by van to hotels and corner shops from Glasgow fruit and veg market stalls. I further enhanced my desire for seagoing employment on explaining I was having wife problems and separation was imminent.

The two big lumps of womanhood elbowed each other on hearing that snippet of my private life. It wasn't too long before I had them sidling over. With swings of their large backsides they shoved the crewmember sat either side of me out of the way, to make room and get close. I had cuddly bottoms planted either side of me. I told them my name was Hamish. They insisted on addressing me as Lovely Jock, and me addressing them as Cara and Tara the lovely colleens.

We were getting along well. I was slipping in a gag or two that they hadn't heard before. The gags either had had them tittering like the proverbial drain or screaming with laughter and telling me that Billy Connolly wasn't the only comic Scotland had on offer. After I bought them a Bacardi and coke each, I had hot breath blown into each ear cavity. Tara blew with a wee bit more puff than Cara and had the larger chest capacity of the two sisters, which hadn't taken me long to notice.

They were both showing breast, were unconcerned about the amount of flesh they revealed, but enough for me to notice. I felt tongue tips tickling my lobes. I fully expected my aural cavities to feel moist tongue. It could have been too public for the Full Monty deep ear penetration. Each time one of them turned, to give a hot blow, I felt a hard nipple ram into my ribcage. More pleasurable than painful, I must admit.

Other crewmembers just grinned at the friendliness shown by their female counterparts. Others nodded their heads and chuckled as if they knew what the girls were up to, had seen it all before. That they were this friendly prompted me to remember and keep my cabin locked, night and day, whether I was in it or not, or they might want *me* to undress them, *me* to blow in an ear or two, three or four.

I don't know if I'm getting more cautious with age. I'm sure situations will arise onboard when I'll find out. All in the cause of a proper investigation, I'd like to assure you.

Apart from the females, as I'd not sailed with any before, their inclusion as crew on British cargo ships coming in the years after my last deep-sea trip. My impression of this crowd was no different to what it might have been on any ship I had joined. The rattle of bottles in the holdall might have an innocent enough presence, might only be water. Older ships tended to have rusty tanks that tainted the drinking water to a light, orangeade colour. Sometimes the ship's fresh water supply was unpalatable to crewmembers.

Two hours seemed to pass quickly. I made two pints of Guinness last. I didn't want to join the ferry tipsy. A blast on the ferry horn and a view from the pub window through the harbour gateway put the ferry alongside with a shore gang making it fast.

I mustered with the crowd and followed them across the harbour and onto the lower vehicle deck. I counted at least two more of us on the walk back. Maybe other crew members joined us in the pub. I was unsure if all were crew. Walking ahead of me, Cara and Tara were more of a brick wall than a window. I don't know if it was intentional. The winter wear of those walking towards the ferry was similar: donkey jackets with hoods up or down, depending on the wearer's preference. No company employee, Gardai or immigration official checked to see who was going aboard.

Lorries were rolling off. It was smoky. I could easily see the foot-passenger walkway down the centre of the deck. I lurched up the internal staircase behind crewmembers sprightlier than I was.

At the top, in an alleyway, and not knowing which way to turn, a helping voice pointed me in the direction of the Second Cook's cabin. The cabin door was open. The man I was relieving had donned his civvies. On seeing me, he pushed past me without a word of introduction and left. He didn't look happy; late for a date or something, I thought. I was hoping to receive gen on galley duties, working hours and anything useful to the investigation.

The cabin was much as I remembered one to be. It had a high bunk atop three large drawers. I hoped I'd be able to sling my arse over the bunkboard into it, my nether regions being a touch heavier than the last time I tried the manoeuvre.

Dim sunlight occasionally shone through salt encrusted porthole glass. The sink with hot and cold running was dirty, the mirror above cracked. The writing desk had drawers beneath. I found at least one cabin drawer I could lock. I needed to secrete my stick and mobile away from prying eyes. If drawers were unlockable, I'd use the padlock I had brought with me to secure holdall contents.

The wardrobe was a tin locker. It had a shelf, a lifejacket on it. The bookrack was empty. The short daybed looked well used. The second cook had stripped the bunk. Clean linen lay on the mattress that looked well slept in with no comfortable sleep now on offer.

I closed the cabin door, slipped off my jacket, shirt, and trousers. I readied myself for galley work, pulling on cook's britches, securing them beneath my overhang with a stout leather belt. I pulled a white T-shirt over my shoulders. A look in the mirror told me I looked like a cook. An old pair of shoes I had with me would do for slopping about in the galley.

I looked for a door key, found it hanging on the bookrack. I locked up and entered the alleyway. I turned in the direction I thought I'd find the galley. Walking past what I discovered was the bar and crew recreation space, a voice shouted, 'You're going in the right direction, Jock.'

I heard a clatter of pans and homed in on the noise. In the galley, I found the Chief Cook. He wasn't one of the men that had assembled earlier on the dockside. We stood around for ten minutes chatting, getting to know each other. He said his name was Sean Fleck, but idiot crewmembers who thought it funny called him Flick. He said he lived in the town of Ballymagilligan, up a height, and could see the harbour from his front room.

He only joined the ferry when he saw it alongside and tied up. This skipper's inability to screw the ferry alongside in adverse weather conditions had caught him out before.

I told him he could call me Jock, as I didn't care two hoots about nicknames. Tommy, the galley boy, appeared. He also lived local. Flick explained to me that, in rough weather, passenger service of galley cooked meals would shut down during crossings, but crew catering went ahead. The cooks leaving on trip off had prepared the crew dinner menu. The cafeteria had a stock of sandwiches that would last until closing.

Before we sailed, we made a beef and vegetable stew for next day's lunch menu. We got a pan of it simmering away for an hour, then lashed the pan to the deck, preventing spillage on the expected rough passage back to Holyhead.

I noticed a hatch to each side of the galley. One served the cafeteria, the other the crew mess pantry, a hatch on the forward end were the doors to a dumb waiter. The handy device allowed galley staff to send food up to the officer's saloon pantry and fetch stores from the cold rooms beneath the vehicle deck up to the galley.

The ventilation skylight was ajar. Wind gusted through the gap. Rain dripped into the galley space, raindrops hissing as they turned to steam on hitting the hot plates of the galley range.

It was quite an old ship and not as large as I'd imagined it to be. The constant smack of it hitting the quay each time a wave pounded into it a sure sign of a rocky night in the Irish Sea, for all onboard. I had never been seasick. I imagined passengers would feel the movement and be 'looking for Hugheeeeee', what hardened sailors called spewing up.

The ferry handled the passage down the buoyed channel of inlet well, pitching and rolling gently. The gong sounded summoning the officers for dinner and crew began appearing in their mess. The feeding was better than I'd served up on deep sea ships. The beef of the main course a good cut, looked tender and rare in the middle.

However, steaks were orders by both officers and crew. The steaks had been part cooked and we only flashed them off under the grill. Could these steaks add up to the missing profit the company was concerned about. Flick prepared the orders without a frown.

I mentioned the extravagance to Flick. He said, 'Anything for a quiet life. Until the company tells me not to allow the crew and officers to have a steak as a menu choice, I'll keep on defrosting them. I know they'll disappear down throats.'

I began to wonder if crewmembers thieved steaks, took them ashore, to disappear down throats at their home dinner tables. I didn't know if I could keep a check on steak numbers supplied, what we cooked for passenger and crew and what remained at the end of a week. If I could, and had the time to do it, the tally up could be revealing.

I took a walk into the cafeteria as the feeding frenzy ended. Tara was out from behind the servery, clearing tables. Lorry drivers and the few foot passengers onboard had taken refuge in the seated area, where comfortable recliners were available. Already, a suspicion of vomit circulated, even though the ferry movement was minimal in the buoyed channel. Tara returned to the servery to collect a bucket and mop.

I returned to the galley as the ferry rounded the heads and began to lurch alarmingly, The motion continuing throughout the night, even though the ferry was doing a reduced speed crossing.

Chapter 12

With a brisk stride Abi mounted the stairs to the senior officer's deck, one hand grasping a banister, the other her baggage. She was sure the captain would be out of his bunk already, smartly dressed, in his uniform, ready to take the ferry to sea.

Dockers had almost completed the shackling of the lorries and trailers as she boarded. Although the sailing schedule was now in disarray, she hoped for a quick turn round. Hauliers would expect it. As trade didn't justify sailing the ferry on a late Saturday night crossing, the company could schedule another crossing then, if a build-up of freight required it. On Sunday p.m., the ferry would resume the advertised schedule.

Abi saw the captain's cabin door was ajar, a hook and eye keeping a permanent space, as she entered the cross alleyway. Instead of dumping her baggage in the owner's cabin, she knocked on the captain's door and waited. Dai Davies' lilting Welsh voice told her to come in. She lifted the hook, entered, then slipped the hook back into the eye.

Captain Davies was sitting at his desk reading a daily paper, in uniform, steaming bonnet already on his head. He turned his head in her direction, stood up and smiled. He stretched out a hand of greeting, which she took and lightly shook.

The captain's cabin had ensuite facilities, a bedroom with a double bed and a day room that he used as his office. The bulkheads were wood panelled with a mahogany veneer, adding a touch of class. Probably the only other cabins on the ferry to have veneered bulkheads were the chief engineer's and the owner's suite. Two picture portholes faced forward, overlooking the bow, and one to the Starboard side.

'I'll make every effort to get us back on schedule,' were the first words the captain spoke, 'but the weather isn't good for the rest of the week, which will hold us back. It wouldn't surprise me if we're late every crossing until it improves. The main engines couldn't offer more speed in a flat calm sea if we were lucky enough to see those conditions. The ferry will never make up time lost if the engineers cannot get any extra knots out of the engines.

'Indeed, yesterday, I couldn't screw alongside in the conditions. I had no tug to help me in Ballymagilligan, isn't it. With the blessing of the Almighty, two hours later, the wind changed direction, the ebb from the inlet decreased and I was able to get alongside the berth.'

'Weather in January is never kind,' Abi said, 'I know you will have done your best. I came up to tell you that our spy in the galley, the second cook, Hamish MacNab, is onboard. He's only signed on for one week. During his time aboard, we're hoping he can spot any theft in our passenger catering facility, in particular steaks. He could also hear gossip of any other goings on, have a nosey around and detect any fiddle that might be going on in passenger bar.

'Fred is tearing his hair out as the profit margins on stock supplied aren't what they should be. Something is going on and, our ill-fated purser, Hugh Rice, couldn't spot what it was. He was also lashing out overtime to Cara and Tara. We're convinced, looking at other catering overtime, it was more hours than they had worked. Then he met his demise when, it appears, the girls were screwing the overtime out of him.

'Rupert is a very experienced Purser. I worry about him, but he is much more robust, in body and mind, to what Hugh was,' she said, thinking at least in one aspect. 'Rupert has our authority to sack anyone thieving.'

The telephone on the desk started to ring. Captain Davies picked up th handset, 'I'll be right up,' he said into the mouthpiece, 'you can prepare to single up, fore and aft.'

He turned to Abi and said, 'We're ready to sail. I must hurry to the bridge. I will see you at lunch. Have you instructed Rupert to tell Cara to set a place for you at my table in the saloon, with me and the chief engineer?'

Abi nodded, 'Already done. I'm looking forward to the curry.'

'I trust my deck officers' experience and abilities to do anything I have to do on the bridge, Captain Davies said, as he escorted Abi from the cabin and locked it. He pocketed the key, then headed towards the staircase leading to the bridge deck. Then he turned, said to Abi, 'Come to the bridge with me. See us leave port. We can have an aperitif before lunch. I will ask my chief officer and the chief engineer to join us in my cabin.'

*

Rupert had sat patiently in his office waiting for Abi to return from her duty to see the captain. As he sat pondering, the entire, worrying, goings on he'd experienced during his first 24 hours as Purser aboard a ferry were his main thoughts: when would Abi grope him, Cara again brush a breast along his face. And he had to suss out incidences of theft. He could deal with any stupid trick played against him he was sure; the events irked him but he thought it better he ignore them until they stopped; showing his indifference he decided was the best course to take.

Shore staff appearing in the foyer disrupted his reasoning. The two clerks flashed cards, confirming they were from the office. They gave him an updated float, which he counted and put in the safe. Then they began uploading cigarettes into machines and disgorged the puggies of their coin take that stretched the coin bags.

The two heavily laden clerks left the foyer as Rupert heard over the tannoy instructions for those not travelling to go ashore at once. Then he felt the rumble of the main engines turn over on a blast of air in readiness to start up.

The captain must have asked for main engines and be on the bridge. Abi would be on her way down! He looked at his watch. It was five to twelve. Lunch was at 12:30. How would she want to spend the half hour until then? Seamen would be fore and aft. A session hearing crew complaints wouldn't take place until later that afternoon. If it didn't suit sleeping crew, it would be later in the day.

Chapter 13

THURSDAY, At Sea.

Rupert felt a slight unsteadiness as the ferry left Holyhead harbour and hit the Irish Sea still disturbed following the night of high winds. The ferry was still well behind schedule. He didn't expect the movement to cause any spillage from plates or the tumbling of cruet sets on the saloon tables at lunch. He was keen to try the curry: to see if it was anything like what his Goanese galley staff served up during his deep-sea employment. He doubted it would. The fresh ground spices and the ethnic recipes they used made a world of difference to the dish. Any of Edinburgh's Indian restaurants in which he'd sampled a curry hadn't come up to that standard.

At 12.30, the gong rang summoning the officers to lunch. Rupert decided to make an early entry, to ensure Cara had set a place for Abi. On cue, Alf appeared to take over duties.

Apart from at the captain's table, seating in the salon appeared arbitrary. Rupert chose the same table and chair to which Bo had ushered him at dinner the previous day. Fergus, a Fourth Engineer, and James, a Second Mate, already seated at the table, introduced themselves. He hadn't met them before; they were on watch during the previous day's dinner. Facially, they both looked in their late twenties. Screwfix and Bo entered the saloon to take seats at the table.

The Chief Mate was a late arrival. He entered the saloon with Abi, the captain and chief engineer, but peeled off to sit next to Rupert. The chief mate introduced himself as Roger and said, 'We got away, but we're still quite a bit behind schedule. I couldn't load her any quicker.'

Rupert looked at the lunch menu. Potage Parmentier was the lunchtime soup. The old, merchant navy favourite, well mentioned in nautical cookery books, Kromeski a la Russe, a sausage wrapped in bacon, dipped in batter and deep fried, with a tomato sauce dip was the starter. Curried beef and vegetables with pilau rice or lamb's liver and bacon with roast and boiled potatoes peas, carrots and onion gravy were the main course choices.

Rupert ordered soup when Cara appeared and asked for menu choices. He noted, on arrival of the soup bowl that the cooks had pureed the soup. He wouldn't have recommended the pureeing. In his opinion a vegetable soup should always have a small but solid lump of a vegetable floating as a part indicator of its recipe.

He had buttered a roll while he waited. The centre of the roll he inspected for any additive. His fussiness produced stifled chortles from his table companions. Tales of Bo's wind up had spread. He also noted the absence of a breast touching an ear as Cara served his soup. From noticing a whiff of her perfume, he was sure it had passed close by.

His soup finished, Rupert ordered the beef and vegetable curry. Cara served it on top of the rice. It didn't look appealing to him, all one plate. It looked and smelled like curry, but it wasn't silver service, how stewards served it on the ships he had previously worked. A plate with condiments in dishes: desiccated coconut, and sultanas, diced onions, diced tomatoes, all carved and looking fresh and mango chutney was already on the table. Rupert littered the curry with condiments, took a taste and gave the curry a pass mark. He had no way of knowing the culinary credentials of the unofficial, overnight cook or cooks.

His table companions were going through the menu and hadn't reached the main courses yet. He heard no complaints from any of them. He wondered if Bo would notice any difference from curries the chief cook normally prepared.

Out of the corner of his eye, Rupert noticed that the captain, the chief engineer, and Abi were all facially rosy, due to a pre-lunch aperitif they'd enjoyed, he thought. The chief engineer was telling jokes. Sporadic laughter interrupted their conversations, the punch lines reached.

When he finished the curry, Rupert worried about it lying heavily in his stomach. He asked Cara to bring him a coffee. 'I never eat a lot at lunchtime,' he said to his table companions. He took the coffee with him, left the table, returned to the office, and relieved Alf. 'I've typed out tomorrows menu cards for you,' he said, before sidling off to undertake other duties.

Rupert thought Abi was taking her time over lunch. The captain and chief engineer had already left and had passed through the foyer to their cabins. When she did walk into the foyer, instead of joining him in the office, she walked towards the hatch, stooped, put her head through and said to Rupert, 'I've just been down to the galley. I've told the cook that he should not serve sirloin steak to any crew member, officers included, unless it is on the menu and that should only be for Sunday dinner.

'I've mentioned to the chief engineer the need of steel wire to secure the galley skylight. He will organise that and have it fitted. I'm off now to the cabin for a quick nap.'

Rupert was glad that Abi hadn't mentioned that he was welcome to join her in the quick nap or any activity preceding it.

Chapter 14

Rupert suddenly realised that he'd not visited the passenger bar whilst passengers were onboard, and the bar was now open for business. He closed the hatch, locked the office and descended a deck to the passenger accommodation.

He walked forward through the seated area without awakening any sleepers and entered the bar. Ten customers congregated in the bar area, half of them sitting at tables or standing at the forward-facing portholes looking out. The other half were standing at or leaning on the bar top. He got his first glimpse of the barman who was conducting conversations in turn with each of those drinkers.

'Boss, I'm Paddy Brennan,' the barman said on seeing Rupert and poked a hand over the counter and between customers towards him. 'We haven't met. Would you like a drink while you're here?' he asked.

Rupert noted the Irish accent and took the barman's hand, giving it a brief shake. 'Not just now, he replied in friendly tones, 'I came along to see how things are going and to find out who worked the bar.'

Rupert took a quick glance at Paddy's face, noticed he had a pencil line moustache, neatly trimmed, the rest of his face clean shaven. His slicked back black hair had the parting in the middle. With gappy teeth he looks a bit like Terry Thomas the actor, Rupert mused.

Then he glanced quickly towards the till front, noticing the box of straws was still in its till-display-obscuring position. He would have the barman report to his office sometime soon. He'd order him to find another place for box. He would tell him that the box's position in front of the till would not inspire passenger confidence that their purchases were legitimate and that complaints might jeopardise his job.

The suspicion that the barman was selling his own drink through company optics he would deal with differently.

Chapter 15

The chief cook was drying his hands with the towel that he held in front of his chest, a worried look creasing his face, the second cook looking over a shoulder, as he stood at the door of the crew bar and said, to the few crewmembers who were sitting around chatting or quenching their thirst, 'That's steak any day of the week knocked on the head. Sundays only. The company personnel officer has just told me. You'd better tell the rest of the crowd that it applies to the officers as well. You've not to expect me to go behind the company's back, have a steak on the sly. To be sure it's an order and that's it. It's the menu of the day only.'

Both cooks heard the groans, the fecks, the feckin' bastards uttered and the words 'Dick isn't going to feckin' like this, not one feckin' bit, to be feckin' sure,' as both cooks turned and headed back to the galley.

'Crew are going to kick up hell on here now. I can tell you that for nothing. I expect I'll get it in the neck,' Flick said to Hamish. They were back in the galley. Flick continued, in an agitated, worried manner, as he went behind the range, picked up a long spoon and began to stir the soup pan vigorously: 'I'd better tell you what the score with steaks has been on here, but. It was my fault that I allowed the crowd to have a steak rather than a choice on the daily menu. I just didn't think it would be that popular.

'Then the officers learned of the allowance and they wanted steaks every day as well. And then, unintentionally, I can assure you, during my early days on here, I left the fridge rooms open after moving meat from the cold room to the defrosting area.

'Under threat, Dick Drake told me to leave it open on trip off days so crewmembers, from either side of the Irish Sea, could help themselves to a steak or two, or anything that took their fancy, to take home with them going on trip off, said I'd get less hassle from the crowd if I did that.

'The Irish side dock has no security and it's lax on the Uk side. I think the security on duty on the Holyhead dock get their share of anything that's going off. The company have obviously cottoned on to a discrepancy in the till takings and the number of steaks delivered. I thought the company would have told me to take steaks off the crew menu a long time ago. That's why I did nothing about it.

'It's done now. We'll just have to live with the decision. How Dick Drake will react worries me. Don't let him coerce you into doing things differently if you value the job on here.'

As Flick ended his woeful tale, Bo the second engineer walked into the galley flicking his measuring tape in and out of its housing. 'Show me where you want this wire secured and fitted.' Hamish thought Bo didn't look happy as he spoke, as if he, too, had clambered down the steps on a food thieving, stew adulterating mission.

*

Dick Drake heard of the loss very quickly. Hearing Flick's words, Ted Higson gulped down the dregs of his pint, brushed the froth from his stubbly chin, raised his backside from the chair and left the crew bar at a fast gallop. He toddled at full speed, the undone laces of his eased-off boots slapping onto the alleyway deck without tripping him.

Reaching the petty officers' cabins, situated at the end of the alleyway, he slid to a stop outside Dick's cabin door. Dick was half asleep on his bunk in full working gear when Ted rapped on his door and burst in. 'The company have fucking banned our steaks,' he blurted out in a rush.

'They've fucking what?' Dick spat out as he was sitting up.

'I'm fucking telling you. Flick has just told lads sat in the pig. Once a week on Sundays. That's it. Menu only from now on.'

Dick swung his legs off the bunk and placed his feet on the deck next to the cigarette packet that he reached for, flicked a ciggy out, lit it, took a puff, blew smoke out through pursed lips and scratched his head. Looking up at Ted, he said, 'We're going to teach someone a lesson. I must get the steaks back on the menu. Steaks every day and to take home for the lads. That's my intention.

'The company isn't likely to change their mind unless we can force them to. Trade is picking up. They wouldn't want a stoppage now. They must be making a nice profit on our backs. I must make it plain to the company that they aren't going to fuck us seamen about.

'Say nothing. We'll have a go at the chief cook first. We'll wait our chance to get Flick on his own, convince him that he will have to go out of his way to please us, like he has been doing since we came on the run. He must find a way to fiddle it in our favour. If he won't leave the fridge door open I'll tell him we want a key to the lock, have a copy made.

'He always goes for a smoke on the after deck before he turns in for the night. One night, in the dark, we'll scare the shit out of him, have a real go at him.' Dick took a quick glance at Ted, looked to assess if he had enough courage for what he had in mind.

Chapter 16

The office phone was ringing as Rupert walked into the foyer. His pace quickened but then slowed. He thought on answering the call he might only hear another raspberry from the lips of a fool. He unlocked his office and entered. The phone was still ringing. He made a grab for the handset and mouthed a gruff 'Yes.'

'Rupert, it's Abi. Can you come up to the cabin and see me. I have something to discuss with you.'

He dropped the handset onto its rest without uttering another word. Abi's request shocked him, even though he suspected something like this might happen. He turned and looked out of the porthole. The sea was calming but not his thoughts. A sea mist obscured visibility to the horizon. Perhaps he had replaced the handset too abruptly, without giving an answer to Abi's question. It was not the call he expected. He would have to explain his abruptness to her. He would have to go and meet her. Abi sounded cheery. She'd understand the annoyance of a raspberry down the phone line and his reaction to it.

Would he have to make a life changing decision: would he make love to Abi if that were what she wanted him for or would he refuse.

He could pack the job in, look for employment elsewhere. Working onboard a deep sea ship, being away from home for months, didn't have the attraction of one week on, one week off of ferry life with extra leave. But then life at home with Sophie no longer offered sex. Yon was out but it seemed readily available in the environment in which he now worked if he was inclined to accept an offer.

Rupert looked at the office directory, dialled the owner's suite number. When Abi answered he said, 'Sorry. The handset slipped out of my hand. I'll be right up. He took a deep breath, settled himself, checked that his tie was straight, brushed down his uniform jacket, closed the shutters and left the office. He looked into the officer's smoke room when he reached it; no one to see him mount the stairs up to the senior officer's deck.

Halfway up the stairs, he looked up. Cara was standing at the top with a tray-load of glasses bound for the dishwasher in the pantry below. No room to pass on the stairs she was waiting for him to reach the deck level. He took the remaining steps quickly, thinking. His get out, if he so wanted one, was standing in front of him. By the time he reached the top he had decided. 'Come with me Cara,' he said, 'I'm on my way to the owner's suite. I can ask if the personnel officer needs your services, see if she has any needs.'

If Abi were after his body she wouldn't want anyone else on earth knowing about it. A rumour spreading around the ship would not be good for personnel relations. He was sure of that.

Rupert knocked on the suite door and waited. He was hoping Abi hadn't draped her naked body across the bed. He pushed the door open when he heard her say come on in. The door open, he saw Abi had her back to the door and was sitting, fully dressed, at the desk, papers from her open briefcase spread across it. 'I have Cara here to ask if you need anything and if you are happy with the suite. A visit now could save you coming up again,' he said to Cara.

Abi turned and looked towards the door. He was sure he read disappointment in her eyes, but she smiled and said, 'Nothing I need, Cara, you've done a good job as usual.

As she turned to leave Cara smiled at Rupert. Was it a knowing one. Rupert stood still, didn't rush into the cabin.

Abi said, 'Come in and close the door. I want you to look with me at these chandler bills and to see if you can suggest a cheaper method of victualing the ferry.' Rupert found another chair and pulled it towards the desk. Abi rose from her chair and moved it to one side, making room for him. He pulled the chair closer to the desk and sat down with what he thought was space enough to avoid a groping hand. 'Rupert, I wondered, with your experience of victualing ships, whether you could suggest an alternative to the ship chandlers that we use.' Abi said, looked up from paperwork and turned to face him.

Rupert said, 'I did have an idea, though I haven't thought it through, that we could buy what the ferry needs directly from supermarkets that have a delivery service. Cash and Carry wholesalers like Bookers have good discounts. Supermarkets like Aldi, Lidl are another cheap alternative. Tesco has stores open seven days a week. Twenty-four hours a day they advertise Tesco Express stores, but not them all are open that long. Butchers local to the docks would be delighted to supply meat that our cooks could carve out into the cuts we need. I could go on, but you will know of these suppliers.

'Together, they will have a greater range of products than chandlers. Chandlers probably buy from them, then add their considerable markup. I know supermarkets deliver orders to householders in Edinburgh. I'm sure these companies would like the extra business.

'You can compare prices with other supermarkets. I'm sure you could strike a deal with one or all of them. As we're in port, on either side, we could stock up on a daily basis, if necessary.' He added, thinking it a bit of levity, 'We would avoid the ridiculousness of the crew rep complaining about horsemeat products coming onboard, though we might have to avoid made-up meals.'

'That's an excellent idea, Rupert, Abi burst in, a broad smile beaming towards him, 'I'll run it past Fred when I get back. He's looking for savings in our operation, even though we're doing quite well freight wise and it's building up so much that we might need a larger ferry or put another on the run. It's all extremely exciting.'

'Is that all,' Rupert said as he rose from the chair and began to move it back to where he found it. 'I want to nip down to speak with the cooks to ensure your instructions will be carried out.' He really wanted to pass by the officer's pantry and let Cara see he hadn't lingered in the owner's suite.

In his rush and on the way down to the lower deck Rupert realised he hadn't mentioned his idea on how to measure spirit sales in the bar.

Chapter 17

'The Boss said hello as he passed the pantry. He didn't say anything more, Cara said to Tara. Both were relaxing in their shared cabin. Family photos and those of favourite singers and actors festooned the bulkheads. A large brassier hung on each of the two coat hangers. On their afternoon break, Tara was lying on her bunk, fully clothed apart from her bra, a book in her hand. Cara flicked off one shoe with the toe of another, prepared herself for an afternoon nap.

'The boss doesn't look the type to fall for any story or service we could provide him in exchange for an overtime payment,' Tara said, as Cara laid her head on her pillow.'

'I think you're right. I think the head office has finally caught up with the thieving that's gone on onboard here. Steaks off the menu except Sunday I heard, and they will be looking at any other fiddle, bastards,' Cara said.

'I'm surprised, Tara said, 'the Gardai haven't been down to the ferry asking questions since Hugh croaked. I wonder if they worked out how.

'To be sure, he gave a great shudder when he went. Maybe it was the second coming. Or maybe that's what he thought and was delighted.' Tara let out a crazy, affected screech of a laugh, before saying, 'We didn't mark him and we wiped the body with cloths laced with worktop Dettol, then swilled that off. I'm sure anyone checking the body will think it was his personal hygiene, showered using carbolic soap. We changed his sheets and dumped them in the laundry to go shoreside. They are ashore. I made sure of that. They wouldn't have found a trace of us, anywhere. An examination of his old fella might have found a secretion of semen. They might think he was enjoying a wank at the time. Let's hope so.'

'Aye,' said Cara, dad wouldn't want us to spoil his wee smuggling business he's got going. Wouldn't want them to start looking too closely at the ferry. Has he said when the next drop off is?'

'Pick up is today. I found his message on my mobile when I knocked off. Usual routine. Bogdan will be expecting one of us at the pub this time we're in port. The football bladder idea with the water activated light attached. I often wondered after blowing that up how long it stayed afloat with the waterproof bag and the dope. Throwing it overboard through our porthole in the dark when we see the torch flash from the fishing boat as we approach Holyhead breakwater sounds simple, to be sure. We're never told if any packages go amiss. The ferry wash could sink it. You know that breakwater snakes out a long way but I never knew it was almost two kilometres long.'

'We'd have heard of any of our drops going missing by now,' Cara said, and turned her face towards the bulkhead, ready to sleep. 'Maybe a pig's bladder is stronger but I'm not going to mention it,' she said.

'Not going to touch my lips. Dad can feck off if he asks us to do that,' Tara replied, then turned over to have her nap.

Cara's spoke, her voice muffled, when she provoked Tara into a response with her jibe from the pillow, 'I bet I'm into the pants of that lovely big bastard Jock, Hamish, before you get your mitts on him.'

'Four cans of feckin Guinness and you're on,' Tara replied, the challenge adding an edge of interest to her voice.

Chapter 18

The rush of crew and passenger lunchtime feeding over, Flick left the galley 'forty winks,' he said as he waved Hamish goodbye. Hamish thought Flick had a worried look about him, sweat pouring from his forehead. Might be to do with galley heat. Maybe more to do with the removal of steaks from the unofficial menu and the flak he'd get from crew following the company's decision.

Hamish put the thought to the back of his mind. Thought of having a rest; he felt tired, his labours after the relative inactivity of detecting and the galley heat catching up with him.

The ferry wouldn't be alongside in Ballymagilligan again for another two hours. Phoning Jenny was out of the question the vessel too far from land. He would call her from the Irish side. Tommy was attending the dishwashers, loading and stacking the washed dishes to dry. He knew to turn the range plates down to low and lock up when he had finished that chore.

Instead of placing his head on a pillow, Hamish lifted the duffle coat galley staff used when entering the fridges and defrosting rooms, put it on and set out on a wander. If anyone asked him why he was in any particular place, then he was orienteering, cooling down, getting to know the layout of the ferry he'd been on for less than 24 hours.

He walked along to the after end of a crew alleyway, dodging the work boots left at cabin doors. He smiled to himself, looked back along the alleyway whilst recalling a deep sea ship on which he had once sailed. The Chief Cook had left his galley shoes outside his cabin door. One morning he found a turd in each of them. 'A dirty bastard,' he said to the galley staff, 'has shit in both of them overnight. What a fucking plaster and the smell to find on wakening up.' The cook had said no more about it, had thrown the shoes overboard and used a second pair he kept. At dinner the next night, as he passed the mess, he heard a crewmember's words and the laughter that followed, 'Who shit in the cook's shoes?'

He'd have to warn Tommy that his boots looked ripe for shitting in.

The cook turned, stuck his head around the door frame, and hollered, 'And who fucking ate it?' His unexpected response quelled the laughter and prevented the floating away of another pair of galley-shoes.

Hamish looked out of the round window on the door leading to what he thought would be the upper vehicle deck. The door was stiff but with his weight pushing it gave. He lifted a foot, placed it over the coaming. He could see the tops of vehicle parked in designated lines on the upper deck, but that deck was a deck below him.

He stepped out onto a half deck that had cover from the deck above. It had room for chairs. Crew could take a chair out, sit, have a smoke, enjoy the weather, when it was a touch warmer than it was in January. The deck run the full width of the accommodation; at the Port end, a view directly over the ferry's side, a life jacket hanging beneath the rail top, at the Starboard end, a staircase down to the vehicle deck an up to the deck above.

He saw no human activity on the vehicle deck. Loaded unaccompanied trailers, secured to the deck, the shackles clanking as the ferry hit a bump. He had heard a crewmember state that the ferry always hit a bump in the middle of the channel, at the border, he said. At first glance, nothing deserved a second look. Hamish took the stairs down, walked towards the stern, along the space between a line of vehicles, including brand new BMWs and Audis, favourite runarounds of the rich Irish.

A Ford transit van had blacked-out rear windows that he couldn't see through. He took a quick look back towards the accommodation, made sure he was alone, tried the door handle. The driver had locked it. He stood quietly for a moment, listening for any movement inside. Nothing. Then dogs whimpered. Then shriller. Maybe greyhounds in stereo his thought. The air vents were open. The dogs were safe. Any illegals in the van the dogs would have licked to death by now. His thought made him smile. Then he stopped in his tracks: what if these dogs were bound for the lucrative puppy market or were breeding dogs bound for a life of misery and cruelty in one of the puppy farms that had been in the news. He'd thought owning a puppy would give his twins pleasure, but would want it reared by good people, in proper conditions. He'd pass on his suspicions to the Gardai when his mobile began working on the Irish side.

He walked to the van front and peered through the driver side window. An overweight man, dark moustache, unshaven face, his snores rattling the interior, was lying asleep along the bench seat, a blanket covering him up to shoulder level. A flask and an Old Paddy whiskey bottle stood on the dash. He clocked the Irish registered number plate that he'd need for his report.

The twin screws were churning away as he looked over the stern, pushing the ferry along at about 12 knots, his guess. A strong, icy breeze whipping past him, cooling him efficiently and he shivered. He couldn't see a corkscrew wake that stretched into the distance but an almost straight one that suggest a quartermaster wasn't on the wheel. The autopilot, which wasn't available on all deep sea ships he'd sailed on, was a more efficient and straight-course driver and must have cut umpteen nautical miles from umpteen voyages on umpteen merchant and other vessels sailing the five oceans and the smaller seas the names of them all he could not recall.

The stern door was securely in the up position and tight against the stern of the ferry. The safe crossing it ensured, his mind turning to the Herald of Free Enterprise disaster where seamen lost their lives as well as passengers.

He was mulling over the disaster on his wander back to the accommodation when an Irish voice from the direction of the ship's Starboard rail said, 'What about you, Jock.'

Hamish turned and walked between cars towards the man, smoke rising from his roll up. Dressed in jeans, t-shirt and donkey jacket, a set of ear defenders hanging around his neck placed the man as an engine-room rating. 'It's certainly fresh out here,' He opened the conversation and chose to stand up wind of the smoker, away from the smoke and sparks shooting out of the roll up in the strong breeze. He clapped heat into hands that had lost heat.

'Sure is,' replied the man, 'I'm Paddy Delaney. I'm on the eight to twelve watch in the engine-room. You'll have guessed I'm a greaser,' and stuck out an oily hand for Hamish to shake.

'I'm Hamish MacNab, second cook. I haven't met everyone onboard to introduce myself yet,' Hamish said, 'no doubt I'll get around to that. I fancied a breath of fresh. These days I'm not used to galley heat, but that will come. And I haven't sailed on a ferry before. I was looking around. Seeing what it's all about. I saw a man sleeping in the cab of that transit van. Carting dogs by sound of the whimpering coming from the back.'

'Drivers shouldn't be on freight decks during a crossing, by rights, but I know a few get away with it,' Paddy said, 'and dogs go in both directions, mainly greyhounds to the mainland, ones that aren't fast, won't make the big tracks like Shelbourne in Dublin. We keep the good dogs, ship out the slower racers, the slow trappers and the fighters. Could be greyhound bitches coming over for mating to a stud dog at a racing kennels over here. We've had cracking stud dogs over here. In demand they were and still are. Sandman, an American import, was a great stud dog we had here. You'll have heard of Mick the Miller, won the English greyhound derby twice, the first dog to do it. He was born over here and owned by a catholic priest, Father Martin Brophy, from the same parish I live in now.'

Leaning over the rail alongside Paddy, they both watched the nearby fishing boat, its tackle hoisted, heading towards the mainland. Paddy said, 'That's a scallop dredger. It's heading in, hold full and extra sacks of scallops on the deck. A good catch by looks of it.

'That one further out is still dredging. He'll have to stop soon, before he reaches the deep, where you Brits dumped all the unexploded ordinance from the second world war. Wouldn't want to raise any of that. But he'll have a chart and know where it's safe to fish.'

Hamish asked, 'What's the largest Irish export crossing on this line.' Paddy looked genial enough, might give something away, if he knew anything at all.

'Bits of this, that and the other, Paddy, said, 'I'm sure. Shippers lock and seal containers and most heavy goods vehicles freight spaces so I've no idea. On open trailers it can be anything from second hand furniture to tractors and other agricultural machinery. Occasionally, quality new cars, like you see, BMW's and the likes, come across, driven on in Holyhead then off on the Irish side. Horse boxes cross when tracks have big races on, both ways. Occasionally we get a tip from the stable lads. It all helps to pay the bar bill if we can get a bet on and we're lucky to be on a winner. Cattle floats travel in both directions, loaded and empty, with lairages either side for the beasts to settle down after the crossings. You'll have met the girls, the Murphy sisters?'

Hamish thought Paddy didn't know much, but he listened intently to his opinion on the sisters, 'A pair of crackers and built like Kerry outside shithouses,' Paddy said. 'Tasty for all that. They'll come on to you, try to get up close. If you're not into a bit on the side, beware, Hamish, but they'll do a turn if you're that way inclined. To be sure, both are a crackin' shag, I heard said, with extras thrown in as well. I've heard it said, though I've not the balls to prove the rumour, that each on their own could ride the horn off an anvil. That's serious shagging in my book.'

'Aye,' Hamish said with a chuckle, 'I've seen them about, not had much to do with them. I got the message. Both have slid into the galley and offered to stir my soup for me.' Paddy might not know too much of interest, but he had to agree with him about Cara and Tara.

'I was trip off and taking leave at the time,' Paddy said, 'but I've not heard anything of interest about Hugh Rice, you know, the purser they found dead in his bunk, the one the new purser sleeps on nightly.'

'Nobody has told me about that,' Hamish erupted, looking shocked. 'What happened to him, was it a natural death or what?'

'Nobody is saying. Maybe no one wants to point the finger. I've heard it quietly said that the Murphy girls were screwing him for extra overtime payments and he croaked during a sexy sesh with them. But don't quote me. I know nothing. I'm sure to be sure that you'll know what not to do if the girls offer to pump your bilges, get rid of the dirty water lying deep in your belly.'

His chatting over, Paddy flicked his cigarette end into the sea and set out back towards the accommodation, letting out a chortle as he went, then shouted over his shoulder, 'Come into the bar and I'll buy you a pint.'

Hamish followed paddy, but declined the offer of pint and said, 'I'm going to have a zizz. See you later.'

Chapter 19

Rupert wasn't asleep as he lay on his bunk. His mind was churning over the day's events. He heard the beat of the engines change and lifted his head from the pillow, threw his legs off the bunk and stood up. Looking out of the porthole he saw that the ferry was nearing the port of Ballymagilligan. He looked at his watch, saw the time was 3:30, realised the ferry was well off schedule, probably wouldn't sail again until 5, even then if the Mate had fully loaded the ferry to cross back to Holyhead. He did up his shirt collar and straightened his tie, lifted his uniform jacket off the peg behind his bedroom door. Brushed his shirt down with a hand, checking for creases, slung his jacket on and buttoned up.

No passengers were waiting for the office to open. He decided to take a walk up to the bridge deck to watch the manoeuvres the captain would make to take the ferry alongside and its docking to the ramp.

He didn't use the route through the officer's accommodation into the bridge, but the outside, Starboard staircase. Reaching the bridge wing level he found Abi standing behind the control panel. She was wearing a duffle coat with the company name on its back, her gloved hands stuffed into the side pockets.

The stiffish breeze was ruffling her hair, making her look even more attractive, a lovely looking woman. What's the matter with me, he thought. How could he reorder his mind? He quickly turned them to the air temperature. It was certainly colder on deck than in the cabin he'd just left. He would have to ask Abi about issuing her pursers with a duffle coat to wear on deck on chilly days.

Abi spotted his arrival, smiled and waved him over to stand with her. 'Captain Davis is on the Port bridge wing for the docking,' she said, 'I didn't want to be a distraction to him. He had problems yesterday getting alongside here. All to do with the ebb tide and the strong wind. Captain Davis assures me that he will not have the same problems with this afternoon's conditions. The hills are quite scenic with the winter flora. On a return passage I'll be able to see them better from this side.'

The ferry had slowed to a safe speed and the captain was making his turn towards the quay. Rupert said to Abi, 'When we talked earlier I forgot to say to you that an optic is available with a counter. I suppose that's what you might order when you consider the idea. They would register every measure taken from a bottle. You would have to have the sales registered by the counter logged and checked against the till receipts. Perhaps that might deter any felonious-minded bar person from placing his or her own bottle on optic to sell, for their profit.

'You could sell miniatures, but bar staff can refill them from bottles brought onboard. It will be a bit more difficult on beer pumps, the froth and the head hard to measure, but a till check will show the expected sales from the kegs. Cans and bottled products should be easy to check. I've not checked how the kegs come onboard from ashore and that they're tamper proof. Adding water to a keg is a well-known trick of the trade. When we get alongside, I'll take you down to the passenger bar and show you the straw box that blanks out the till window.'

Rupert and Abi left the bridge wing when the ferry was close to the quay, dockers were hauling ropes ashore and placing the eyes over the bollards, the docking going to plan.

No passengers were in the bar when he followed Abi into the area. A light was on behind the bar grill. Paddy Brennan wasn't on duty tidying up or tilling up after the crossing.

Abi walked up close and peered through the grill. 'I see what you mean,' she said, 'a handy device a straw box. Say nothing until I suss out the availability of the optics you mentioned and I'll order up when you tell me the total you'll need. We'll cut out another fiddle if you're correct. You'll have to keep your eyes peeled and watch that the barman hasn't another devious ruse up his sleeve.'

Abi walked towards a porthole and looked out over the fo'c'sle. 'We're alongside. Ropes are on the bollards and the deck crowd and are standing down,' she said without looking back. She turned and said to Rupert, 'I've decided to get off here and miss a round trip. I'm going to speak to our office staff and then I'm going to drive towards Dublin in a company car. This afternoon I'm going to visit hauliers who use our service and others that don't. The don'ts I'll encourage with a good price to use us. The users I'll tell of the excellent service and freight rate they get from us.

I'll be back for our overnight crossing to Holyhead. I'll see you then,' she said, gave Rupert a bewitching smile, sidled up close to him, her eyes locking on his, reached for his hand, she pressed it and said, 'You've been good for me. I hope you'll like working on our ferry and stay for a long time.'

Chapter 20

Thursday Afternoon in Ballymagilligan

Hamish had dozed for about an hour his batteries not quite recharged. The rumble of the engines had changed; the vibrations roused him from his slumbers. He wiped a smear of condensation from the porthole glass, raised his head from the pillow and took a quick glance through. The ferry was turning, manoeuvring alongside the dock and ramp had begun.

He lay until he realised he could now use the mobile to call Jenny. He had dressed and was ready to prepare crew dinners. He threw his legs over the bunk-board. His feet on the cabin deck he slipped them into his galley shoes, reached a hand for his bag laying on the day bed.

He searched beneath yet to use clothing for the mobile, switched it on and waited for it to spring to life. A signal showing, he was about to search for Jenny on his list of contacts when a text appeared in his message box.

The text was from Aunt Jean, the code Commander Dewsnap had given him for the Gardai commander contact. The wordage was quite terse: Fleck, the chief cook, goes ashore to his home once daily whilst ferry is in port. Does he take anything ashore with him or fetch anything or anyone back with him. Delete this text once read.

Not to my knowledge, Hamish typed back. I've been aboard less than 24 hours. The weather has been bad. The ferry is no longer on schedule. It's been hectic onboard but I'll keep my eyes peeled. I have a worry to report. I thought I heard dogs whimpering in a sealed Ford transit van. It could be dogs or children whimpering, might be worth checking out with a stop. The vehicle registration is Republic. I wondered, if they are dogs, could they be heading for a puppy farm, a problem I believe you might be interested in or to pass to your relevant animal protectors. Human trafficking you'll be interested to check that out.

He added the plate number of the van. Sent the text then deleted it.

He telephoned Jenny. She answered quickly. Briefly he told her what the job entailed and how happy he was to be back at sea. She wasn't pleased that he was happy to be away from home. She said to him in a raised voice, 'Don't get any ideas in that direction. I want you home every night to keep me warm in bed, you big lummox. Have they told you how long you're going to be away? The bairns are missing you already.'

'If I discover anything report worthy in a week onboard I'll let the company clear things up, or the Gardai. I'll call you every couple of days if

I get a chance. Give John and Jessie a big kiss for me. Now go away and leave me alone to do my job, well job for the Job. Any worries you cause me will make me want to wind down with ten pints of Guinness a night and I'll be twice the size I am. I'll look like a Michelin man. By the time I get home I'll be smellier than usual.'

Jenny quickly put the phone down.

*

Hamish returned to the galley. He was on his own when Tommy said he'd have to go for a crap. Tommy was passing through the door on his way out when Cara shouldered him out of the way on her way in. 'Smells like you've shit your pants,' she said on passing him.

Hamish saw the collision, heard Cara's words. Smiling, he walked from the galley range to the veg preparation table. He had a knife in one hand and a bag of carrots in another, ready for carving enough into a julienne for the main dinner course on a chopping board. He hadn't time to place veg and knife on board when he tensed. He felt Cara's arms encircle his waist, fingers interlocking, squeeze his stomach muscles and then tickle him. He felt her breasts push into his back, the nipples hard. He felt both hands slide down towards the front of his trousers. He wasn't going to allow her fingertips to tickle any lower. He wasn't going to allow the encounter to continue. He knew what she was after and maybe steaks on the side to take home.

'If you don't piss off and leave me alone, I'll report your conduct to your big sister to see what she has to say about it,' Hamish said, his head to one side, without turning around.

'She'll be feckin jealous that I got my arms around you first and she wouldn't be as gentle with you as I am,' Cara said, breathed hot air on his neck and continued tickling.

'Look,' Hamish said, lumbering his body round a full body turn, the knife in one raised hand and a half carrot in the other. Cara's arms slumped down to her side her crestfallen face asking why? 'Flick will be here any minute,' Hamish continued, 'and you shouldn't be caught doing anything like this,' Hamish said, trying hard to suppress a smile, though his lit-up eyes he couldn't hide.

'I often wondered what shagging a Jock was like, especially a big, well hung bastard like you. I've never had the experience, big boy,' Cara said, looking Hamish in the eye. 'If you think you could fit me into your bunk alongside you, any way that suits your taste, just let me know. I'm into headhumping and I know you'll like that,' Cara said, licking her lips, looking for the look of joy on Hamish's face. Not seeing signs of imminent romance she turned, smiling cheerily over her shoulder, Shouting to Hamish as she walked out of the galley, waggling her arse as she went, 'It's your choice and It'll be the best experience of your life. Your choice.'

Headhumping, Hamish said to himself. That must be the Irish equivalent of a blow job.

Chapter 21

'Flick walked jauntily into the galley smiling broadly. I'm off home to see the wife. I'll be back in half an hour and it's a bit chilly out. He lifted the duffle coat from the hook behind the door and shrugged it over his shoulders. Hamish was doing a circuit of the range, checking the pans and stirring the soup when he replied, 'I wore it this afternoon out on the after deck whilst taking a breath of fresh air. It will keep you warm.' He watched Flick as he buckled up the toggles on the coat. Warmly clothed and ready to go ashore, Flick picked up two tinfoil wrapped packages from a side shelf and stuffed one in each pocket.

Flick saw Hamish's look and said, 'It's a steak for the wife's tea and one for the local Gard. Say nothing. Certain crew members would string me up if they found out. The company order of steak only on a Sunday will have got up their noses. None of them will be happy if you get my drift.'

Hamish wasn't about to say anything. Fleck's perk was small potatoes. His task was to detect the presence of bigger fish swimming in criminal waters, though he hadn't seen or heard anything report worthy, except what he thought might be dogs, during his first 24 hour on board the ferry and he hadn't investigated anything yet. 'I'll put the roasts in the oven for dinner. When Tommy appears, I'll make sure he prepares the rest of the veg. I'll make up a pint of mint sauce. That should be enough,' Hamish said, as he headed for the galley fridge where the rolled leg of lamb joints were relaxing.

Tommy returned from his toilet break. 'Hamish, he said, 'what drink do you have in Glasgow bars? That Smithwicks we have in the pig is pish. It goes right through me. Sitting in the cludgie I thought I was passing a flight of starlings; pebble dashed the back of the pan, I did. I wish they'd get rid of the pish.'

'Not strong enough for you, eh?' Hamish asked.

'You'll be used to a Scottish pish brand, I reckon,' Tommy fought back.

'Our bars are much better and drinkers worldwide appreciate our beer, better than the pish beer your local dishes up, and on here. Guinness is totally different. The black stuff. I'd always drink that in an Irish pub or a pint of Caffreys if I could get it on draught and at 5 percent.' Hamish responded.

'You're talking pish,' Tommy replied.

Hamish thought he'd tease the lad with one of his tales. 'I want you to picture the scene in the Glasgow bar I supped a pint in at Christmas. I was with my mates, Angus, Donald and Jamie. We were standing at the bar. It was a city centre pub. A pint of Tennent's lager with a nice head rested on a beer mat in front of each of us. A world renowned lager is Tennents and the tipple of choice for Scot's lager drinkers. The Tennent's Extra lager is five percent and a bit too strong for me.

'Angus is a tight arse. He started a conversation saying, "My local out in Paisley is better than this dump. Duncan, the barman, always has an offer on for us regulars. If I buy a whisky, the next is free, no matter the cost, a Low Flyer, or other on optic."'

'A Low Flyer?' piped up Tommy, sceptically.

'You wouldn't know the Scottish slang, Tommy. It's a Grouse. Grouse Whisky. You'll probably have the birds on Irish moorlands, like us. They're a heavy bird, small wings and tend to fly a bit on the low side.'

'Maybe we do,' Tommy said, his thinking cap on, trying to imagine the feathery things.

'My mate Donald responded saying, "That's, fuck all. Aggie, the woman working my local bar in Baillieston, has not only great tits she also gives the choice of two free house malts if you buy one 25 year-old Glenlivet."

'Jamie pipes up with his I'm going to beat these two fockers response, "In my local in East Kilbride, if you buy one vodka, Martin the barman gives the 2nd, 3r, 4th, 5th, 6th and 7th free. Then you can go upstairs and have a shag."

"Wow," Angus and Donald respond in unison. "Has that actually happened to you, Jamie?" "No," spouted Jamie, but my sister has been lucky several times!"'

'You're having me on, now, Hamish. Bars can never be that good,' Tommy said, eyes narrowed, giving Hamish another disbelieving look.

*Cara avoided an argument with Tara by not telling her that she was lighter on her feet than her. She let Tara take the walk to the pub to pick up the package from Bogdan.

They were both on their feet, readying themselves for the duties that would begin when passengers or freight drivers started to embark. Tara was strapping on her bra and struggling to fit her ample breasts into the holsters, as she often called the cups. She shouldered on a blouse, did up a button but left a view of her breasts, hoping it was tantalizing, then raised them on an arm and worked the holsters into her working tunic. Her overcoat hung on a locker hook. It looked weighty but she shrugged it on to her shoulders with ease, checked the collar was outside and the inside concealed pocket that her dad had called the poacher's pocket was empty.

She heard the docker's whistles as she walked across the lower vehicle deck but her eyes were on Flick as he walked off the ramp onto the dock as she walked onto it. Flick was in a hurry, he never looked back, never thought a pair of eyes were on him.

Outside the dock gate, the uniformed Gard sat waiting in his police car, listening to chatter on the radio. Flick always brought him a steak on a Thursday when he was aboard. Flick and Gard Tim Devlin were on first name terms, they were neighbours, drinking pals in their local, had often chatted over the garden fence, shared the same pew at Sunday mass. Their kids walked together to and from the same school.

Flick saw the car sitting with Tim behind the wheel. He veered towards the passenger side door, opened it, sat in, pulled the door closed and belted up. The Gard pulled away.

Tara walked through the gate as the car turned right. She had a clear view of the driver and of Flick placing a silvery package on the dashboard top. Gard and Flick weren't looking her way.

Tara wondered what might be in the package as she walked towards the pub. Was it Flick taking the piss by supplying the Gard with a steak, or was it something different, something else and worth knowing about. Either way, Flick wouldn't want to learn that she or any crewmember onboard knew of his wee game or his bigger one.

Her dad would know what she should do about it. She walked past the pub, took her mobile from a pocket, chose dad from her contacts and called him.

Her dad was into dodgy dealings but he thought he was still beneath the Gardai's radar; thought they knew nothing about him and wasn't on their watch list. The entire family thought he was small enough in the gangster game and smart enough for the Gardai not to know of his operation. He certainly didn't want his daughters to fall foul, implicated in any of the dealings he had with the crystal meth and crack cocaine makers in the Republic and the North. But his girls had both insisted on helping him along in this small way.

He had told them that the package they took to the mainland for him was a cannabis resin block and not any serious drug. They had agreed to do that, they both liked a toke at home, occasionally skunk grass or an E. The package they took onboard and dumped through their cabin porthole into the sea for the mainland fisherman to pick up, in the waterproofed carryout container and primitive though effective flotation device, with a water activated light fitted, was a hard, seriously addictive drug, not what that the girls or their father thought they were delivering.

Paddy Murphy received a courier fee from the traffickers, which he pocketed, never passed a share on to his daughters, though sometimes bought them a Baileys with ice in their local pub.

Dad didn't answer her call. He could have forgotten to take the mobile with him or he was having a shite, Tara's thoughts. She walked back to the pub and entered through the bar door.

Bogdan smiled in her direction as he pulled a pint of Guinness for the only other customer, a tall, well-dressed man, his roving eyes clocking her, looking her up and down.

Might be Gardai, her first impression. She would be careful.

I'll have a half pint of the black stuff, when you're ready, barman, Tara said, not wanting to convey any fraternity with Bogdan.

His pint pulled and paid for, change in his pocket, the customer placed a hand on a stool, dismissed sitting on it, waved the hand at it, thought it uncomfortable, uttered an 'Ach', and wandered into the lounge and stuck a Euro in the bandit. He didn't seem interested in drinking in the bar or clocking the bar area, his back turned towards it.

Tara opened her coat. On other occasions that act had been the signal to Bogdan that she was ready to receive the package and its floatation contraption.

Bogdan lifted the hatch, opened the half door. Tara turned, her coat opened, thrust her belly into the gap. The customer was still facing the bandit. Bogdan slipped the package into the poacher's pocket and was quickly behind the bar again, the half door closed the hatch down, and he giving the bar top a wipe with a cloth as if nothing had happened.

Tara supped her Guinness quickly, buttoned up her coat. The poacher's pocket was to the front of the coat. The package invisible to prying eyes hanging beneath her ample bosom.

Tara left the pub. She tried to contact her dad as she crossed the dock, her ear to the phone, her eyes to freight movements. No luck with the call. She would keep trying.

Chapter 22

Hamish had checked the dry stores but couldn't find any goose fat which was a proper chef's smear to apply to potatoes for roasting: it had a high smoke point, crisped nicely and gave the potatoes a better flavour. Tommy was having a break and wasn't on duty to tell him if they had or ever had any. He had to make do with beef dripping. He was plastering a tray of spuds with the fat when Flick, who had been away an hour and a half, not the half-hour he said, when he walked into the galley, hung the duffle coat up behind the door and asked, 'How are we doing?'

With a smile on his face Hamish looked at him, said loudly, 'We've,' then continued in normal voice, 'roasted the lamb nicely, the joints are resting and still slightly pink in the middle. The soup's simmering, the boiled spuds are ready to go on the range as are the sprouts and carrots. This tray of roast spuds is ready for putting into the oven. I've gravy to make. The mint sauce is ready. The fruit cocktail and ice cream is an easy sweet to box off. What have you been up to?' he said, still smiling, until Flick's reply wiped it away.

'My wife has MS. She's in a wheelchair, getting worse, Flick said, looking downcast. 'Her carer didn't turn up today to make her lunch. I fried the steak I took off and made her a sandwich. My kids are old enough to tend to their mother's needs after school and until the carer comes in again to put her to bed. I cannot take the risk. I cannot leave it to my kids anymore. I've decided that this will be my final week on here. I'm going ashore. I'm taking the job as chef in the local Gardai canteen. The money will be less, but enough to live on and I'll be home every night. To be sure, now, keep that quiet. I don't want the hassle of telling everyone the reason. I want to slip away quietly. No piss up with the lads or anything like that.'

Hamish felt a pang of sympathy for Flick and said, 'Take all the time off you need whilst I'm onboard. It won't be a worry to me. Just be happy in yourself that you're doing the right thing for your wife and family.'

Tara stuck her head through the galley door as she passed on her way to the cafeteria, bawled in Flick's direction, 'I saw you feed the pig when you were ashore, remember that when I ask you for a steak, won't you?'

Flick stood, mouth wide open, on the point of replying, but Tara wasn't for hanging around for an answer.

'Feck! How the feck did she notice that. She must have followed me off,' he said, raising his head in thought. Flick turned to Hamish and said,

'My neighbour is the inspector at the local Gard station. He waited outside the dock gates in the Gard car to see if I was coming off, to tell me I had the job. I gave him one of the steaks I took off. I was so pleased to hear the job was mine. The bitch probably saw me hand it to him. Feck! I'm glad I'm leaving but I'll soldier on until then. I'll go and tell the purser, put my notice in. I'll be gone by next Wednesday. Cooks are looking for jobs the likes of ours over here, and over the water, too, but you might find yourself chief cook sooner than you thought.'

Chapter 23

Thursday late afternoon sailing from Ballymagilligan.

The ferry had loaded trailers carrying various pieces of freight and others as empty flats. It took extra time for the Tugmasters to take down the ramp and negotiate into vehicle deck lanes. The cooks had wiped down the galley. Hamish was sitting in the pig enjoying a pint of beer, sitting at a table with Flick as company. A crib board between them, they played the popular seafarers card game. They agreed to wager a round of drinks on the best-of-three outcomes and he was giving his hand full attention.

The tv set Suddenly began to lose the picture of the 6pm newscaster. 'That's us going round the head. We won't get a picture until the back of 9 if we're lucky, fifteen for two and one for his knob,' Flick said and moved his marker along the board, adding three to his score.

The back of 9 arrived. The stable picture on the tv as the ferry berthed at 8:30. Hamish and Flick were still cribbing. Having lost three rubbers each they'd supped six pints. The beer was a low in alcohol and had little effect on them.

*Late evening in Holyhead

On the ramp in Holyhead, the duty mate discharged the ferry and loaded it quickly. Holigan Express put to sea at 10:30. The deck crowd that had been at stations to let go the ropes for the ferry leaving port entered the bar, Dick Drake and his sidekick Ted Higson amongst them. 'I hope you two aren't playing for high steaks, get it,' Dick said, causing members of his gang to show their appreciation of his pisstake with braying laughter, his sidekick Ted braying loudest of all. Crew members from engine, deck and catering departments using the pig joined in the levity. As well as concentrating on the cards dealt, Hamish was also listening to the craic. The majority of the crowd then sat around the tv and watched a film on DVD.

Hamish and flick were still cribbing. 8 pints each they'd supped. They'd played for the entire crossing, supping contentedly, having the odd conversation and banter with others. Pigs afloat were always like this, Hamish thought.

*Ballymagilligan to Holyhead crossing, early hours Friday morning

The rumble of the main engines starting up signalled shortage of freight and another quick turnaround. Flick said, 'It's gone one o'clock now. I've had enough. I'm going for a piss, have a fag on the after deck, then to my cabin to sleep. It's been a great night. We'll have to do this again. I'm halfway pissed. I'll see you for breakfast.'

The film had ended and Hamish was alone in the pig. He stowed the cards and crib boards on a rack. Flick wasn't in the heads when he went to urinate.

In his cabin Hamish undressed quickly, hoisted his frame over the bunk-board onto his bunk, took a look out of the port hole, saw the beam of the lighthouse on Lobhar Island flash over the sea, drew his curtain, switched his bunk light off and laid his head on the pillow. He was quickly asleep.

Chapter 24

Saturday on passage to Holyhead

Rupert had turned in at midnight, read two chapters of the Wilbur Smith book Hungry as the Sea. He'd found it in the officer's bar library and looked interesting. He put the book on the floor beside the bunk, switched his reading light off and settled into what he hoped would be untroubled sleep. He had no idea how long he had been asleep when he felt the moist, warm, rasping piece of flesh slide across his face, and something that tickled his nose. And what was the strange odour? The sensations startled him. He opened his eyes, thinking he'd find Abi standing alongside the bunk, naked, ready to leap on him and tear off his pyjamas to get at him!

In the darkness of the cabin he couldn't make anything out. Abi must have gone directly to the owner's suite on returning from her tour of Republic haulier offices. Surely, it couldn't be her. He groped for the reading light switch on the bulkhead behind his head.

The light revealed the reason for his alarm. A goat stood looking at him its bloodshot eyes rivetted on him over the end of its nose. It had a long beard, well developed horns and floppy ears. He thought it a billy. What! How and why were the words that shot into his head as the goat let out a baa. Then he realised: this was another of Bo's, or another ferry joker's, idea of mischief or plain childish humour, having a laugh at his expense.

Irked that an officer might have been the prankster he looked down at the carpet. He saw no goat faeces, could not smell any, no disgusting goat jobby to clean up. He was at least pleased about that. He picked up the book from the floor and placed it under the pillow. The alarm clock that stood on the bedside cabinet he had knocked over. He righted it, didn't look at the time but wondered how long the goat had been in his cabin..

He knew he'd locked the door to the office and closed the bedroom door. Someone onboard must have a key to the office! Must have gained entry, opened his bedroom door quietly, shoved the billy in. He swung his legs off the bunk and stood up, quickly, fearful of a butt on the nose. He'd no idea how long the animal had been in his cabin. He had to have it removed quickly and safely before it started causing damage or shitting all over the bedroom carpet. It was prancing and practicing head butts.

He detected a main engine rumble. The ferry was still at sea. He strode into the office, closed the bedroom door behind him, caging the goat. He put the office lights on, picked up the telephone handset and dialled the bridge number.

The watchkeeping second mate whose name he had learned was Peter, answered. 'I've one of your goats in my bedroom. Would you send a goatherd to round it up and remove it, please.'

'You've a what?' was the surprised retort. 'Does it have a name?'

'It's a fucking prank, he spat into the mouthpiece, 'I'm sure it could be one of Bo's immature ones.'

'Ah. Got it. Keep it in the bedroom. I'll send the lookout to return it. We are carrying goats in a trailer parked on the top deck. It will take a minute or two as he'll have to find a length of rope to tether the beast. Keep it happy. Sing it something soothing from The Sound of Music.' He let out an off key burst of the hills are alive with the sound of music, a guffaw and a baa.

Before Peter could put the phone down, Rupert, somewhat irked, had hollered into the microphone, 'We have too many fucking jokers on this ship. Get it out of here, pronto!'

Chapter 25

The bridge lookout knocked on the office door and entered smiling. He wrestled with the kicking and butting goat; fought the beast to place the rope around its neck and succeeded. Uncontrolled, still obstinate, doing a merry dance, the seaman dragged it from the cabin, as if it had taken a liking to its surroundings and didn't want to leave them.

The goat smells Rupert improved with a whiff of a perfumed aerosol before he slipped beneath the duvet and tugged it over his shoulders. He tossed and turned. He reckoned later that it took him an hour to settle into sleep. He had overslept. During the upsetting experience with the goat he had accidently touched the alarm cancelling button on his bedside clock and had slept on past its seven-thirty alarm setting. When he looked, the clock had stopped at 00:46, the battery and the cover keeping it in place were missing. The clock couldn't have awakened him anyway. He hoped the goat hadn't eaten them. He looks around the deck next to the bunk but didn't see the battery or the cover. Maybe under the bunk, he thought. A job for Cara. He didn't fancy getting down on hands and knees to search for them and it was getting late. He should be up and on duty.

The rapid knocking on his office door took him through to answer it. He put the lights on and pulled the door open.

Hamish was standing outside looking in, his concern and booze-bleary eyes noticeable. 'Flick has gone missing,' he erupted. 'I last saw him as he went for a piss and a smoke before turning in. Must have been just after one in the morning, just after we sailed from Ballymagilligan We've checked everywhere. I don't think he's onboard. His hasn't slept in his bunk. Tara, Cara and Tommy are up and about. They helped me look in his cabin and all the usual places. I opened and checked the storerooms the fridges, the laundry baskets and the rubbish bins. Looked down the side and underneath the freight parked on the main deck, Tommy searched the top deck.

'Where are we? Are we alongside?' Rupert asked, then realised he could hear the engine rumble.

'We're on our way back to Holyhead. We did an overnight crossing to Ireland. Looked like we loaded what was waiting on the dock. Must have been a quick turnaround. I cannot see a great deal of freight on the decks,' Hamish replied, 'and we must be on a slow speed crossing, probably down to one engine, because we're not alongside yet. Maybe engineers were working on the engines. We're still a distance from port.'

Have you contacted the bridge? The Mate on watch will have the ship thoroughly searched.

'Thought I'd speak to you first, Hamish said. 'Flick didn't seem worried about anything. In fact, as you know, he has a job ashore to go to and was looking forward to finishing. He wasn't in the heads when I left the pig. Must have been having a smoke. I saw the flash from the lighthouse as we passed the island on our Port side, whatever name it has. I don't know the exact time that was.'

'I'll dress and head up to the bridge,' Rupert said, turned and went back to his bedroom.

Rupert took the outside staircase to the bridge deck. He followed James the other second mate in through the Port wing door. The time was just before 08:00, when the watch changed. He interrupted the heads down over the chart table when he said, 'Mr Fleck, the chief cook, we cannot find him onboard. Can you organise a proper search of the ferry?'

Both deck officers looked directly at him. 'Has your staff searched for him?' was the first question James asked.

'Yes, they've searched all the places you'd expect. Hamish, the second cook, said he saw Mr Fleck going for a smoke before turning in, not long after we sailed from the republic, said he was with him in the pig when we sailed. And he saw me yesterday to give in his notice. He has a job to go to ashore, I believe.'

James said to Peter, 'on your way down, knock up the skipper, put him in the picture. The same with the chief officer. I'll give the bosun a shout and have him start a search.'

Dick Drake was in Ted's cabin updating their conversation of the night before when he heard his telephone ringing through the thin bulkhead wall. 'Remember what we agreed. When the Gardai interrogate us, as I'm sure they will, keep it simple. We saw Flick walking aft on the freight deck, until he disappeared behind the freight, and we never saw him again. If they ask you why you were in tears when we came back into the accommodation tell them it was a funny joke I told you, about paddy being in love with a donkey. They won't ask you to repeat it, they'll be thinking it bestial. If you have to tell them, tell them you've forgotten the punchline. If they do, tell them it was something to do with it having bigger knackers than you. Have you got that?'

'Aye. I think so,' replied Ted.

'I'd better take this call. My phone hasn't stopped ringing.'

*Captain Davies was at breakfast in the saloon, the first piece of crispy bacon of his normal full breakfast plate speared on the fork. The morsel was in mid-air as Peter spoke, standing to the far side of the table, 'The chief cook has gone missing. He went for a smoke on the afterdeck, just after we sailed. That's the last anyone saw of him.'

Captain Davies tossed his cutlery back on the plate and left the table quickly for the bridge, Peter scurrying behind him. He knew the captain would need him for the search.

The bosun had already reported to the bridge when Captain Davies strode in with urgency. 'All spaces, all spaces, you hear me,' he said in a rush. Call the chief engineer on his cabin phone. He should be up and about by now. Tell him to report here and quickly. If we don't find the cook onboard, then we must inform the Irish coastguard for them to start searching. If the poor man has gone overboard, the sea temperature what it is, he wouldn't have lasted long. Now bosun, turn all your men to and start them searching. When you've looked everywhere, all cabins, all deck spaces, all freight vehicles, nothing missed, report back to me, here, on the bridge. Now go to it. James, enter in the log that I arrived on the bridge at 08:05.'

The chief engineer walked into the bridge, still in his slippers. 'I've rang the engine room, he said to the captain as he approached. The engineer on watch has started searching all engine spaces, the purifier flat, the tunnel, under the plates and the steering gear space. That shouldn't take too long. We have the watch greaser and the storekeeper to help him. I've ordered the second engineer to finish the work on the engine worked on overnight in case you're going to turn her round to search our course and need the extra knots?'

'As soon as we're sure he's not onboard,' the captain said. He cannot have slipped ashore. The second cook said he was onboard when we sailed. Let's hope he still is. If he's gone overboard I pity him, and his family. He has kids of school age' He turned to Rupert and asked, 'Who broke the news to you, Rupert?'

'As you've heard, It was my second cook,' Rupert replied. ' Mr Fleck hadn't turned to for breakfast duty. Hamish checked his cabin. He hadn't slept in his bunk. The galley staff search did not find him in any of the places they searched. Apparently, both cooks had a lengthy cribbage and drinking session in the pig and turned in late. Hamish thought it was just before we passed the island to our Port. He saw a flash from the lighthouse. Mr Fleck said he was going for a smoke on the crew after deck before he turned in.'

'The captain ushered Rupert towards the chart table, placed a finger on the chart and said, that is Lobhar Island. It was to our Port side in the buoyed channel when we sailed. James, check the chart and estimate the time we passed the island. When we have that information, and we cannot find the cook onboard, I can tell the Irish coastguard where to search I'll wait until the bosun reports back, then I'll have to tell Abi.'

The first report that the bridge received was that the lifebelt that hung on the crew after deck was missing.

Chapter 26

The Order of St Lazarus Priory on Lobhar Island had not looked after leprosy sufferer since the 1950s; the contagious disease beaten with the discovery of antibiotics. The colony building was now known as The Priory. It was still the present-day home of the Order, whose brethren had once cared for the inflicted. Today, the Order served a different purpose: any man who needed solitude and the healing of prayer that the Order offered could take a break from their hectic world and find peace on the island, in the company of monks who had devoted their lives to the different cause. Although the Order insisted on abstinence from alcohol during the guest's stay, they didn't mind the smokers amongst them taking a smoke outdoors, after prayers.

Father Gideon also liked a smoke but did not wish to publicise his habit, lighting his only cigarette of the day as he took a walk after the Abbot's midnight lectures, Bible readings, catechism studies, prayers and intoned chants. He was enjoying his nightly puff on his way to the island edge that faced the navigable channel for larger vessels using the port of Ballymagilligan. He found the inspection of the colony's lobster pots advisable following the passage of larger vessels leaving or entering the port. The wash created by those vessels had occasionally ripped the pots from their marker buoys. He would count the markers to ensure they were still in position. Lost pots becoming unattached to the markers and the rope to raise them meant tasking a monk skilled in the use of an aqualung to reattach the rope and the chain to hold the markers to the pots and ensure they both were in good condition.

It was a little after 1.30 am when he arrived at the island edge and cast his eyes towards the pot markers that reflected dimly the flashing light fitted atop the main channel marker buoys. Scattered dark clouds hid the best of moonlight. It was of little use. As was the beam from the lighthouse that skirted the buoys to hit the sea further out. Earlier, a Ferry had negotiated the channel outward bound, its whistle heard as the chanting, the last act of the midnight chapel sessions, ended. The wash was still lurching the buoys marking the channel. It was then that he saw the figure clinging to the buoy twenty yards away when the flash of a buoy light briefly illuminated the whiteness of a face. Could the person be alive? Was it a body? Had it somehow become entangled with the buoy anchoring chain? Questions he had to know the answers to.

Father Gideon didn't hesitate. He increased his stride and ran down the narrow pathway that an earlier age of brethren had cleared of rocks, onto the sand of the short beach. He tore at his habit, dragged it over his head, threw it onto the sand, plunged into the sea and strode out through the shallows towards the buoy. He knew of the steep, underwater incline to the depth safe for the larger vessels and needed for the pots to trap lobsters. He would have to swim the last few yards. The tide was on its ebb, but Gideon, swimming a strong and urgent breaststroke, reached the buoy and tread water. He saw a man and the lifebelt he was clutching. The man let out a moan and then a weakening, strained cry of. 'I'm feckin' freezing.'

The coldness of the water was getting to Gideon as he let the lifebelt drift away and swam, holding the man's head above water, using his legs and one arm until he reached the shallows. His feet on solid ground he was able to drag the man to the beach. He saw the man was naked apart from a white T-shirt, was of slight build, wasn't overweight. Gideon placed his hands beneath the man's armpits, hauled his cold body off the sand. He was limp, incapable of standing, looked all in. Gideon lifted him, stooped, turned him so his face would hang downwards, forced him up onto a shoulder, his belly resting but probably not comfortably, stood up and began a slow lope up the incline of the beach towards the priory.

In the communal hall of the building a fire roared in the great hearth of Donegal Sandstone, monks and guests gazing into the flames. It was a nightly game they played musing over visions they thought the dancing flames created, as Gideon bustled in with the rescued man hanging loosely over a shoulder. 'Quick,' he cried, then took a deep breath, 'I need blankets to wrap this poor soul in. I found him clinging to a buoy.' Gideon laid the man down in front of the fire. 'He is unconscious, I don't know how long he's been in the sea, undoubtedly he's suffering hypothermia, but still breathing. I see hope for him. Someone get the first aid box and dress that nasty cut on his side.'

Blankets were quickly at hand. Monks and guests began wrapping the man.

Gideon was deep in thought as he stood shivering. What should he do next. Perhaps find a dry habit and put it on when he realised he stood naked, losing his undergarments during the swim. Before going to his quarters he said, 'Find all the hot water bottles you can, boil water. Wrap the filled bottles in towels and place them around his body under the blankets. This will help him to a speedier recovery. Massage his limbs. Warm him up, get his blood moving around them. Find him a set of undergarments. They must have come adrift in the water. I'll be back after I find another habit. Then

I'll get his rescue reported to the authorities.'

The priory Abbot, Father Jacob, hated his name: residents looking for peace and prayer had occasionally and absentmindedly referred to him as Father Jack, an odious character in a comedic and much loved by the public TV sitcom, set on the fictitious Craggy Island, that he had watched only once. Father Jacob had slept for only 30 minutes when Gideon knocked on his dormitory door, opened it and switched on the room light. The only mobile phone allowed in the priory, Father Jacob, for safe keeping, locked in the office safe. It was for official use only or to order the craft that delivered the needy and took away the cured, and for the use that Gideon now required of it: an emergency.

Chapter 27

Captain Davies lifted the bridge phone and dialled the Owner's Suite number. Abi's sleepy voice said, 'Hello.'

'This is Captain Davies. We have an emergency, Abi. Our chief cook is missing. A search is underway. The bosun hasn't reported back on his search yet. If he's not onboard, we will turn around and retrace our course to where we were at the last time anyone saw him onboard. I will report our emergency and our return to the Irish Coastguard Service and the Gardai.

'I'm almost awake,' Abi said, 'I will dress and come to the bridge. Do what you have to do. Informing the coastguard early might be vital. I do hope you find him onboard.'

'I have a feeling about this,' Captain Davies said to the officers assembled on the bridge. 'I'm going to turn her about in readiness to make a hasty return trip. Chief, can we have both engines if needed?'

'Bo has changed the faulty fuel injectors and a cylinder head on that engine. He should have the turning gear out ready to turn the engine over on air and start her up. Ready when you are, I'd say, but he'll shut it down again if he has to.'

'James, have you worked out our position when the cook was last seen onboard?'

'We must have been manoeuvring in the buoyed channel at the time, on standby at half speed.'

'How long at full speed to get back to that position?'

'We've only steamed 34 miles since Full Away. About three hour at full speed, I'd say. But we're lucky to do 12 knots on any crossing in bad weather. 15 knots we can do but only with a brisk following wind and the sea up our stern.'

'Phone the engine room and ask for the other engine, please. We must do all we can, even if we find the cook on board. Chief, can you give me any extra revs on our return?'

'I'll give you all I safely can,' was the chief engineer's unchanging reply.

'I'm not wasting anymore time. Turn her round, James. Set a return course. Get the bosun up here. Tell him I want lookouts on Port and Starboard bridge wings, another overlooking the bow and two on the monkey island.'

'Rupert, I know we only have three passengers onboard but use the bridge PA and make an announcement, explain to them the circumstances of our course change. And phone the galley, ask the cook to send me up a round of bacon sandwiches. I didn't finish my breakfast.'

*Hamish stayed in the galley during the search. The workload for he and Tommy in the preparation of lunch had increased. All other catering hands had been turned-to to search. His lumbering presence and woozy head wouldn't aid them to a quicker conclusion. But Flick's disappearance worried him. Flick was looking forward to ending his sea service, not ending his life. His wife needed him home more often now than ever; her illness, MS, had no medical resolve that he knew of. His nearby presence and new job would be ensuring to her that help was only a short distance away and he'd be home every night.

Hamish's opinion that somehow Flick had gone over the side he kept to himself. That he suspected the bosun had something to do with the disappearance he also kept to himself. But why? The only grouse that the bosun had was the reduced steak availability and that was a management decision.

When the captain's order came in for bacon sandwiches he prepared them himself, and the extra order for the purser who had also missed breakfast, wrapped them in foil and sent Tommy to the bridge with them.

'Mr Drake the Bosun has reported in. The search has not found Mr Fleck on board. The Gardai have called on the RT channel and asked us to continue into port and dock. They want to come on board. The Coastguard Service obviously have told them. They probably want us to confirm his disappearance and them investigate it,' Captain Davies told Abi when she arrived on the bridge.

'Poor man. So sad,' Abi said in reply, a tear forming in the corner of an eye. 'I will have to see his family, if the outcome is tragic, but I will wait and speak with the Gardai when they board,' Abi replied, 'you can come with me Dai, and you, too, Rupert.'

'I don't know the protocol that the Gardai work to, Captain Davies, replied, 'I don't know if they will let the ferry sail or keep us here until they conclude any investigation they might have in mind. I hope not. We've lost enough time this week.'

'I will ask them to sail with us to Holyhead and back if they need to investigate,' Abi replied.

Captain Davies nodded his head in agreement, offered Abi his last bacon sandwich, which she refused. He strode towards each bridge door, carrying the plate with him, checked for a lookout in position and cast an eye to the monkey island where he saw two lookouts, one on either side, looking forward and to the side, each scanning the sea that he saw the force 4 moderate breeze was ruffling.

*Captain Davies rang the telegraph for the engineers on watch to reduce engine revolutions to "dead slow". The ferry had passed the first buoy of the channel into Ballymagilligan port. He told James to enter 10.30 a.m. in the logbook and asked the bosun to muster the seamen not already on lookout to man the rails of the top cargo deck and to keep their eyes peeled until docking.

Rupert headed to the galley. Hamish would be busy, run off his feet, though under the circumstances he didn't expect to hear any complaints from crew because meals were late. He found Hamish and Tommy hard at it preparing veg. Pots were simmering away on the range and whisps of smoke were filtering from the ovens.

Chapter 28

When the ferry reported the man overboard emergency to the Irish Coastguard Service they had already completed a rescue mission. They had informed the Gardai of the situation. A medivac helicopter had picked up Mr Fleck and dropped him off at the Ballymagilligan cottage hospital. He was safe, recovering but doctors were monitoring his irregular heartbeat.

The ferry had reached the entrance to the buoyed channel when Hamish shot along to his cabin, locked his door, found his mobile and tapped the Gardai commander's number. A cultured Irish voice said, 'Commander Dunlevy, have you anything of interest to tell me? It's Hamish, isn't it?'

'Aye, we have a man overboard situation.' Hamish said.'

We know about that already. A monk from the priory on Lobhar Island scooped your man, Mr Fleck, out of the sea. He saw him cradling a buoy and swam out, in the dark, to rescue him. I reckon it was a brave effort and the monk should receive praise, awarded a medal. Have your captain speak to the British Minister for shipping. I will send the same to our Minister for Transport.

'Mr Fleck was lucky. He was suffering hypothermia. The monks got him wrapped in a blanket and warmed up. That helped him survive, I'm sure. He's a bit befuddled, in a warm hospital bed now. He's receiving the best of care but doctors are worried about his heart. They think he has suffered a heart attack which he might not recover from and he has a weak, erratic pulse. They also found a stab wound to the right side of his chest. It wasn't life threatening, they say, but to me it suggests whoever put him in the position of danger, they wanted him to die.'

'It's a relief that he was rescued,' Hamish gasped, 'his disappearance was a big worry for me. I hope his ticker holds out.'

'We've told your captain to continue into port. We haven't told him of the rescue. It's all a bit suspicious to me and we want to find the underlying cause of it. If it's an attempted murder enquiry we might get someone to blab before the perpetrators have their alibis arranged. We will board when you dock. I'll be leading the investigation. The ferry can then continue to Holyhead. I'll interview you early as you worked in the galley with the man.

'Do you have any suspicions, Hamish? Mr Fleck has said that he was having a smoke and looking over the ship's rail when two men grabbed from behind. He thought two men must have been lurking in the dark for he never saw or heard them approach. He didn't see their faces and they never spoke a word. Said it all happened so quickly. They held him over the rail by his legs and trouser belt. He thought the only reason for a threat on his life was if he didn't put steak back on the daily menu. This sounds very trivial to me, not like a gangland turf war or drug lords falling out over territory.

'Then he said he felt the knife going in, His unlaced boots slipped off of his feet and his legs out of his galley working trousers. The perpetrators couldn't hold him. He landed in the sea, the wind knocked out of him. He heard a splash close by as his boots and trousers hit the water. The lifebelt that followed his gear he was able to grab onto. One or both the perps must have known the danger they were putting Mr Fleck into when they threw the lifebelt. The ferry wasn't at full speed and he watched it sail away. He doggy paddled towards a buoy and held on to it. He said hitting the water stunned him. I suppose he didn't know what to do next and he was only a short swim from safety. That's where the monk found him. An incredible stroke of luck; a miracle Mr Fleck had.'

'I've nothing concrete,' Hamish said, 'but I'd have a chat with Drake and Higson, they're two seamen in the deck gang. They're scousers, union minded, though I don't know if this is a union ship. I'm not a member of any, but they are militants and trouble. I thought Drake was off his rocker when he accused the company of using horse meat for beef steaks. Acting what in my days deep sea was known as sea lawyer. Higson, basically, is Drake's lackey. I'd work on him first. He doesn't look the stronger of the pair, physically or mentally. A sandwich short of a picnic as we say over here, a slate missing from the roof and the underfelt irreparably damaged.'

'See you soon,' The commander said and rang off.

Hamish couldn't tell him that Flick was supplying a Gardai inspector with steaks. Didn't want Flick to lose the job that he surely now wanted more than ever, though he'd be needful of another pair of kitchen boots and working trousers. Perhaps before he left the ferry he'd start a collection to get Flick kitted out for shoreside cooking.

Back in the galley, Hamish found Cara, Tara and Alf chatting to Tommy. None of them were smiling 'What do you think has happened to Flick, Hamish?' Alf asked.

'I don't know. I hope for the best. If he has gone overboard, then rescued, it will be a miracle. How any of that might have happened, we'll have to wait and see.' He wasn't going to spoil Dunlevy's investigation by letting his news slip. He too wanted the perpetrators caught. He noted that the girls were tearful and had the build to heave a slight figure like Flick's over the ship's side, though Flick thought it two men. He walked between them, put an arm around Cara and Tara and pulled them close. They responded, turned and threw their arms around him. Alf, head bowed, followed the girls as they left.

Tommy sidled close to Hamish, the galley to themselves, and said quietly, 'I saw Dick and Ted following Flick out onto the deck as I went to my cabin last night, well early this morning. From my cabin, I heard Ted sobbing when he came back and Dick telling him to be quiet. I didn't think anything of it but I do now when we haven't found Flick.'

'Keep that to yourself until we get back to port. In fact, don't tell anyone what you know. We could have onboard those who don't like a grass and who could make your life hell,' Hamish told him, 'keep yourself occupied in here. We've enough to do to put on a decent lunch menu. Put enough spuds in the peeler, fetch another sack of carrots up from the store. Open three tins of peas. We'll put mince and tatties on for lunch. We can make that quickly. For dinner, the roasts are ready for the oven. I'll make a start on the entrees and sweets.'

*Rupert had returned to the bridge after making his announcement but left together with Abi when he realised the navigators didn't need him and he'd get in the way of the lookouts. Abi said, on their way down the stairs, 'I must tell Fred what has happened on here and bring him up to date. From our home, he can see Holyhead harbour entrance and will be wondering why he hasn't seen Holigan Express arrive yet. The news will shock him. He'll not want reporters buzzing him for a quote if the story has leaked that far. I'll see you later. I suggest that you put your wife in the picture. You wouldn't want her to worry unduly.

She would probably start thinking of a scrabble word to use that describes the events, like catastrophe, worth 18 points and more depending on the placing of higher value letters if she could fill in the gaps between and extend the letters already on the board, Rupert thought, but didn't tell Abi. 'We should get a strong signal now so I'll do that,' Rupert said.

They parted on the deck beneath, Abi to her owner's suite, Rupert down another flight to his office. The first thought he had as he settled in his chair was to ring the galley, to see how Hamish was coping with the extra workload. The call was unanswered after a minute. Rupert locked up and descended a deck to the galley. Hamish and Tommy were both occupied as he looked through the door. He couldn't blame them for not answering the phone. Hamish was carving meat from a roast leg of ham for the salad course, Tommy removing eyes from peeled potatoes. He walked towards the worktop where Hamish was busy and said, 'Simplify the menu today, if you have to. I cannot see any complaints coming under the circumstances.'

'We'll do our best, Boss. What's happening anyway? We're on our way back, I heard.'

'We're almost in. We'll be alongside shortly. We'll have visitors in the shape of the Gardai and maybe someone from the rescue services to make enquiries. I don't know how long that will take. If they want to speak to you, I'll turn to here to help out. Just let me know. The Gards will probably need feeding as well.'

'The fat bastards amongst them would eat the decorations off a hearse,' Tommy said and cackled loudly at his own humour.

Chapter 29

Commander Dunlevy of the Gardai Special Detective Unit was striding from the linkspan onto the ramp when Roger, the Chief officer, greeted him with a cheery smile and a handshake. It was 11-05 a.m. Dunlevy was one of the younger Gardai commanders, tall, slim, a keep fit freak. He was wearing a casement green tweed jacket, brown corduroy trousers and brown brogues. His stride kept placing him a foot or two in front of the chief officer as they crossed the vehicle deck. 'I see you haven't much freight onboard.'

'Weekends are always light,' Roger replied, 'I see unaccompanied freight on the quay now. We'll load that and take it across this trip back. We have space available on both decks.'

'You'll need to take me directly to your captain,' Dunlevy explained.

'Follow me. He's waiting in his cabin. Have you a team you want to board, too,' Roger asked.

'They're in a van outside the dock gates. I'll get them onboard as soon as I explain events to your captain. I take it my car is ok parked up next to the office?' Dunlevy asked.

'If it's not in anyone's way it will be fine,' Roger told him.

'Captain Davies met Dunlevy at his cabin door and ushered him inside. Both sat at the cabin desk. Dunlevy said, 'Your cook, Mr Fleck, is safe. A monk from the priory on Lobhar Island rescued earlier this morning. He alleges that crewmembers held him by the legs, over the side of the ferry. He has a knife wound and he slipped out of his working gear and fell into the sea. He could not name the perpetrators or didn't want to. Said he was looking out towards the island, hadn't time to turn, then his face was towards the ship's side and it happened so fast. The monk saw him holding onto a buoy and swam out to drag him ashore. Fleck is a lucky man. In my book, an offence was committed in our waters. We should recognise the act of heroism on the part of the monk.'

'It is wonderful to hear of Mr Fleck's rescue. I had given up hope for the man in the water temperatures at this time of year. It must have been quite a scary ordeal for him. I hope he didn't suffer unduly or have traumatic aftereffects,' Captain Davies said, holding his hands together as if in prayer.

'Poor man,' continued Dunlevy, 'he thought he was a gonner. As he reached the buoy he heard voices, mournful, keening, echoing over the water from a distance. From the chanting voices he mistakenly construed it was banshees, spirits coming to grab him, propel him into the netherworld. Then he saw a giant on the beach. He said he was about to give up at that moment, didn't realise rescue was at hand.

'We still have folks that believe in the existence of little people, banshees, goblins, leprechauns, imps and the likes. Of course, what he heard was the monks doing a late evening thing. The chanting and racket probably sounded like a dreadful wailing, mournful beyond all other sounds on earth. I'd have needed a stiff tot of Irish whiskey after hearing that. Would probably have scared the shite out of me, had I been in the same situation. I believe if you're troubled with drink you can enter the Priory and the monks will dry you out, put you through their Holy wringer. Must be a painful process and one I will avoid, for sure.

'The Gardai will have to investigate this. As I see it, it was either a prank that has gone wrong or an attempt on his life. The knife wound suggests that the cook's life was under threat. We will have to interview all crew members and any passengers travelling across. We can do this here, with the ferry alongside the berth, or we can do it as you sail back to Holyhead. I take it that the ferry will cross and return to Ballymagilligan later today. That should give me enough time to suss out the gravity of the situation and hopefully arrest any culprits. Hamish MacNab, who I know you are aware of and the reasons for his insertion onto the ferry, has already given us a lead. I'd like you to keep that quiet. If I can get a confession early, all the better for all concerned.'

'It would suit the company, I'm sure, if you can sail with us. You can use the officer's bar for the interviews. Our watchkeepers will need consideration. You will have to factor in their off-watch periods. They could be sleeping. That way the ferry operation can continue as normal. When and with who would you like to start.'

'If you can provide me with a crew and passenger list, I can start as soon as my inspector and search team come onboard,' Dunlevy said and stood up. 'We will do a cabin search as well. We have the authority to do that. If you can give me a pass key, the team will be able to open all doors in their own time. We'll show consideration to those crew members who will be sleeping after watchkeeping overnight. I don't know yet what we might be looking for, but you never know.'

'We should have a pass key on the bridge,' Captain Davies said, 'though I cannot recall seeing it. The officer on watch would know. I'll ring the bridge now and ask. I'll get it brought down to you now if they have one.'

Chapter 30

The driver of the Gardai transit van drove the vehicle over the linkspan onto the ramp at a rate of knots that loading officers would frown upon. Freight lashed to the vehicle deck slowed it somewhat but tyres squealed when it braked and halted close to the staircase up to the accommodation decks. The transit back doors opened fully and six overalled Gardai leapt out. The inspector and driver ran the few steps from the cab to join them. The five men and two women of the search squad formed a column, the inspector leading them towards the staircase doorway. Taking two steps at a time, they mounted the steps and quickly arrived to meet Dunlevy on the first deck. It would be their first search area; the crew cabins, the galley, cafeteria, passenger bar and seating.

A craft of the Gardai Water Unit working out of their base at Santry, situated to the north of Dublin, turned, came alongside, a Gard dropping its anchor. The vessel would remain close the ferry until it sailed, alert Gards watching for jetsam or illegal activity of any sort.

Complete with the knowledge that the two stewardesses onboard were of interest for other reasons, Dunlevy ordered the two female Gardai to search the stewardesses cabin. He handed a pass key and the crew list to the lead searcher, the cabins with sleeping watchkeepers marked 'do not disturb'.

Cara and Tara were sitting in the cafeteria drinking coffee. They heard the heavy patter of feet and the voices of the Gardai. Together, in a boisterous mood, they left their coffee on the table and marched, arms swinging to their cabin. They saw the male Gard standing outside and the backs of the two female Gards as they stepped through their cabin doorway. Tara in the lead, Cara behind her: they didn't fit into the alleyway space walking together. Their stride lengthening, they reached their cabin door, turned, looked in, and hollered in unison, 'What the fuck do you think you're doing in our cabin?'

'We're searching your cabin. What the fuck did you think we were doing,' the lead Gard retorted, in language he suspected the girls would understand. 'We have instructions to search the ship and that includes your cabin. We're looking for the missing cook. If you want us to find him, fuck off out of here and let us do our job. While I'm at it, what do you know about the missing cook?'

'We know as much as you do, by looks of it,' Tara threw back at him. 'Not a feckin lot. Crew have already searched the ferry and didn't find him. You should be looking elsewhere. You're only covering ground already searched. We're as keen to see him found safe and well. He's a popular crewmember. So feck off. You can see we haven't hidden him in here.'

'We'll look round to make sure you have nothing of his stored away. So just fuck off and let *us* get on with our job,' the Gard said, pointedly, swinging a thumb along the alleyway in the direction they came. 'I'll cross off your names as seen but make a special note of your concerns as well as your belligerence, abusive and foul language. We might have to interrogate you further if we find anything incriminating, link you to the cook's disappearance. So stick around. Don't leave the ship.'

Cara had to get a word in and hollered, 'I've heard all about you lot planting stuff, incriminating the innocent. We'll stand here and watch while you search. Make sure you don't try to stitch us up.'

The lead Gard snorted his distaste at Cara's words and moved to the side so that they had a better view of the search. Scribbling onto his work pad he said, 'I've got all that.'

The cabin search was over. The view through the porthole was of no interest to the searchers. Tara mouthed to the two retreating female Gards, 'Watch the door doesn't smack you on the arse on the way out,' as she threw the door closed.

Back in the cafeteria, their coffee was cold. Tara became barista and renewed their cups to their liking. Sitting together at the table Tara said, 'It was a good idea of yours to hang dad's package out the porthole on that bolt.'

'Aye, and to lash it safely with gaffer tape so the wind doesn't catch it and blow it away.'

*On early ships with cabin portholes, sailing tropical waters or in summertime across any sea, with little in the way of comforting air conditioning in cabins, crews used a five gallon oil drum, cut lengthwise, in two, to fashion a wind scoop. Fixed to the open porthole, with the window open, the hollow of the scoop caught air and forced it into the cabin space, giving a degree of cooling, when the ship was on passage.

Tara and Cara might have wondered why the bolt was outside theirs. Now it had saved them. The searchers left the porthole unopened, hadn't looked out.

Chapter 31

Commander Dunlevy sent a Gard to find Hamish and fetch him for his interview. The Gard took Hamish directly to the smoke room, said nothing on the way. Using a kitchen towel, Hamish wiped his hands as the Gard showed him into the smoke room. He shook Dunlevy's hand. Dunlevy introduced him to Inspector Power who had closed the door behind him. Hamish noted that the inspector was the least tall copper he had ever laid eyes on; probably a fast track entrant into the Garda, who had never patrolled a walking beat, probably overly officious, who now sported a drill sergeant approved haircut, a neat short back and sides.

Dunlevy sat in the comfiest chair in the room, his coat draped over its back. He had a tape recorder on a table to his side, a microphone on top. It was recording as he opened the conversation and ushered Hamish towards the chair facing him. 'What do you know that will help us?' he asked.

'Very little, I'm afraid,' responded Hamish. This is Saturday. I joined on Wednesday. I've had two full days on here and I haven't had a chance to poke my nose into anything. Today has been hectic in the galley planning feeding for all onboard with a man short. I didn't want to overreact and look suspicious.

'I've kept an open ear for anything said. I've already made you aware of that and reported what I thought was the transportation of dogs into the republic. If I know anything about dogs, the dogs would have licked any illegals to death. Words I have heard crew talking about is that the purser, Mr Sewell, has been snooping about, seen looking keenly through the passenger bar grill at the optics. Someone spotted him entering the cold stores. It was probably a crewmember who locked him. Then Tommy ran down to the store flat released him when he pressed the alarm. I don't know what that was about, could've been a prank, or a warning of a sort. I don't know what his brief is on here, other than running the hotel and catering side.

'I was relieved when you told me on the phone that Mr Fleck is safe and well. Surely, he must have known who the perps were? The galley boy, Tommy, told me he saw Drake and Higson follow Mr Fleck out onto the deck when he went for a smoke. From his cabin Tommy heard Higson weeping on the way back and Drake telling him to quieten down.'

'We'll interview that pair individually,' Dunlevy said, 'don't want to rush it. We could do it on the way back. Wouldn't want them to scarper on reaching the mainland if they cotton-on to what we know. If evidence comes our way before then we will arrest them. Of course, we have cages in our van. We'll hear what Tommy has to say later. I'll fish for something more concrete first. Before we have a chat with Drake and Higson I'll question other crew members, see what they have to say.

'We're already checking all crew with CRO at Scotland Yard and our Criminal Record Office to see if anyone signed on has a record. We believe children smuggling has been going on for years. Arrests of smugglers has shown they were using ferries to and from South Wales to the republic. The children were young, small, easily concealed in a boot or under a blanket on the back seat of a car or lorry. Usually, they were Thai or Filipino, the girls very pretty. It's a sin that we're desperate to stop.

'Next time snooping about on deck, you might be lucky enough to save a child from the sex game or from a life of slavery. We found puppies in the van you reported. We traced the reg number and followed it home to the Finglas area of Dublin. We found ten kilos of cocaine hidden in the dog bed. The van driver is under arrest as are members of the gang he was delivering to. Of course, the driver had no idea the dog bed was stuffed with the drugs, he says. Stay safe. Vicious people of Organised Crime gangs, on both sides of the Irish Sea, are behind that trade. We have you to thank for what has turned out to be useful information. Good work. Good result.

'Corroboration is a handy tool for the lawman over here as well. I'm sure you know that. We only have Mr Fleck's account of what happened to him. He was rambling a touch, talking of banshees coming for him, when we spoke to him. He was, perhaps, suffering a trauma after his ordeal. He could change his story. We have an inspector at the hospital who is waiting to talk to him if he improves and his heart doesn't give up. Any change of story whilst I'm onboard I will hear.'

'The ferry will leave soon for Holyhead; the weather has calmed and it's a nice day for a sail. Captain Davies has informed us in the last ten minutes that a build-up of freight on the other side means the company wants a return crossing today. With a bit of luck, and an easily obtained confession, we could return happy to the Gardai station tonight and have perps in court on Monday morning.

'If I arrest anyone I'll lock them up in the van and have Gardai on duty. I'll keep Drake and Higson until later. They seem the more likely perps, but I'll need to hear from someone who actually saw the dreadful deed and are prepared to give that evidence in court before I can nick anyone with confidence. Unless, of course, they admit to the crime or tell me it was an accident, a prank that went wrong, or I can drag a confession out of them that they intended to murder Mr Fleck. We'll see how it goes.'

'Most crew speak English day to day but I do hear words spoken between crewmembers that I don't understand and suspect is Irish Gaelic,' Hamish said. 'I'm sure, that anything Irish speakers needed to say secretly, whilst any British member of the crowd onboard was near enough to eavesdrop, they would use that language.'

'A difficult one,' Dunlevy said, 'but you still have a good set of eyes and the nose to sniff out a criminal, if everything your commander tells me about you, is true, or *fior*, as we say in Irish. I trust you will be diligent for the rest of your stay. I'll try and get a decent bottle of Irish whiskey to you before you leave, something to remind you of your time here.' With his speech over, Dunlevy stood up, took Hamish by the hand and shook it vigorously. 'I'll let you get back to your galley. I'll see you again, no doubt, but certainly before we leave. Say nothing yet about Mr Fleck's rescue.

'You will have your chestnuts in the Met, stories that have circulated for years, as we have over here,' Dunlevy continued, whilst standing up. 'This is the latest I heard circulating throughout the Gardai. You can tell it when you return to your station. At 23:00 one Saturday, the Desk Sergeant at an up-country Gardie station received a call that thieves had committed burglary at the home of farmer Paddy Mulgrew. The sergeant radioed night-shift motor patrol constables O'Toole and O'Reilly to attend the farmhouse at Honeysuckle Farm. Their knock on arrival had the farmer answer the door.

In the farm living room, the constables' saw dust on furniture, around spots where certain objects had once stood.

Constable O'Toole took out his pocketbook, proceeded to question Paddy. O'Toole asked if the stolen articles had stood on those spots and jotted down the ones that were.

Paddy said yes and listed Mulgrew's loss. The bastards had taken his flat screen TV, his sat box, his I-pad, an alarm clock gifted by the farming community for his charity work. That is hard to believe. Farmers in my experience are as tight as a duck's arse and are probably instrumental in finding out if that's a fact. Anyway, his mobile phone and an old pair of trousers, or dung hampers as farmers know them, with small change in a pocket, went as well.

O'Toole asked Paddy to tell him how the perpetrators managed to gain entry.

They came in through the back door, Paddy said and that the thieving bastards had taken the door, the hinges and the screws, left him with a hole but no door and he couldn't see the door anywhere out the back in his potato patch.

Whilst Constable O'Reilly checked the back door. O'Toole asked Paddy if he had anything else to report.

To be sure, said Paddy. His eyes were rolling upwards into his head by this time. He said he had a big pan of colcannon and a bigger pan of beef coddle on the stove and that the bastards had shit in both pans and he had to throw half of each pan away.'

Hamish laughed along with Dunlevy and Power as the chestnut ended and thought that it would receive loud guffaws when he told it to his squad mates.

Returning to the galley Hamish was also thinking that Commander Dewsnap might have tried to impress Dunlevy that he'd sent him one of his best detectives but he had never used those words when congratulating him for his part in thief taking successes.

Chapter 32

Dick Drake had checked with the captain if he needed lookouts for the trip across to Holyhead and was on his way down the inner staircase from the bridge. Two steps up, before he reached the engineer's alleyway, he spotted the trousered legs of a cook leave the officer's bar. Had to be Hamish, he thought, as he briefly halted his progress to think what he should now do. The officer's bar door closed as he stepped into their alleyway. Acting out the thought that came into his mind, he knocked on the bar door, pushed it open and stepped inside. 'You'll be wanting to speak to me,' he said to Dunlevy, lifting his head up from a note pad that he'd written on, surprised at the intrusion.

'You are?' Dunlevy asked. Both he and the inspector eyed Drake, who stood slapping the pair of dirty gloves he held in one hand into the palm of the other.

'Mr Drake, the bosun. You'll want to interview me before long. I was on my way down from the bridge. I saw the cook leave. Thought I'd save you the bother of looking for me. I'll have duties when we sail and work to do after. Thought I'd get it over with now.'

'Very decent of you, I'm sure, Mr Drake. We'd have got around to you later today as you have an important job on the ferry but take a seat and we'll get down to it now, not keep you too long away from your duties.' Dunlevy thought he'd have interviewed Tommy the galley boy by now but that would have to wait, now he had Drake sitting in front of him. 'Right then,' he said, 'this is Inspector Power. He will sit in on all interviews. We will record them too, for our records. What can you tell me about the cook going missing?'

'I was taking air on our after deck along with Ted Higson, one of the ferry's ABs, when we saw Mr Fleck walking aft down the Port side of the top vehicle deck. He was smoking as he walked but looked a bit unsteady on his feet. He had played cards and drank beer with the second cook for hours. The pair had supped a dozen pints each, I'd say. They were in the pig for hours.'

'Interesting,' said Dunlevy, 'did you see him near the ship's rail, hanging on to it for balance, anything like that?'

'It was a calm night, no pitching or rolling. His movements were noticeable. He wasn't walking in a straight line.'

'Ted Higson will confirm what you saw, Mr Drake?'

'He noticed his staggering first. He drew my attention to it.'
'How long did you stay on your outside deck?'
'We were outside for no more than five minutes.'
'Do you suspect that Mr Fleck fell overboard?'
'We didn't see him walk back and he hasn't been found onboard.'
'Do you think drink played a part, if it is found that he went overboard?'
'I'd say so.'
'Anything else you can tell me?'
'R, the purser, he has been snooping around the ship…..'
'What do you mean. Is R a nickname or something similar?' Dunlevy cut in.

'R, when you place it in front of his surname is exactly what us in the crowd think of officer classes and I don't know what game he's on. R Sewell sounds about right to me. He might be a company stooge, looking for ways to save them money. He might have followed the chief cook aft, got into an argument with him, told him that he was giving away too many steak meals. I can see that being a reason for pushing Mr Fleck, whilst he's unsteady on his feet, and he can't stop himself from going over the side.'

'I'm sure Mr Sewell will not appreciate your intended description, be up in arms when he hears it, but did you see the purser at any time on the after end of the ferry?'

'No, but he could have been waiting down aft. He would know the cook likes a smoke before taking to his bunk.'

'What you've told me, Mr Drake, is remarkably interesting. We will consider what you say. We have your testimony on tape,' Dunlevy said, pointing to the recording machine. 'You can go now. We'll have your sidekick along and hear his story.'

Chapter 33

Tommy was standing back from the range, watching steam rising from gently bubbling pots, when Hamish walked into the galley. He walked forward on seeing Hamish, picked up a long spoon and began stirring the mince, simmering on a lower heat. 'Soup and lunch main course and veg is all ready for delivering to the pantries.' He had noted Hamish's questioning gaze and responded. 'The entrée of sardines on buttered toast the pantry hands can make up. They have a toaster and can openers. They've done that before.'

'Open three tins of fruit cocktail and put the pantry containers in the fridge to cool,' Hamish instructed, 'bring cartons of ice cream from the cold room and put them in our freezer here in the galley. Make up a cole slaw, slice tomatoes, and wash a couple of lettuce. A cold meat salad might be of interest to those who don't fancy mince. I hope we don't hear too many complaints.'

Hamish stuck a finger into the mince and tasted it. 'Stick two oxo cubes in the mince and give it a good stir around,' He told Tommy. 'The tastier the better. Less complaints to listen to. I'm going for a quick walk aft. I've never really had a good look around the harbour and I need to cool down.' He didn't mention that he'd a mobile and was going to talk to his wife Jessie whilst he walked. He didn't know if the UK media had broadcast the missing cook emergency. If they had, he didn't want Jessie to worry.

'The Gardai put you under the grill, made you sweat, did they,' Tommy asked, smiling.

'No, only routine questions. I could tell them nothing because I know nothing. They wanted to know Flick's state of mind. That was all good, I told them, though I still cannot believe he has gone. I just fancy a breath of fresh air. I'll be back in five minutes to help you with lunch and knock up dinner.'

Tommy said, 'Before you go, I must say that, in my time on here, this is the worst menu this galley has ever served up to passengers, officers and the crowd. Could you not have done any better than mince and tatties, Hamish? You have sailed on deep-sea ships of greater tonnage than ferries, must have had a bigger crowd to feed.'

'It's an emergency menu. We've put out what we could in the time, without Flick to guide us. And we've been looking for him for all morning. I learned to be creative as a seagoing cook, but maybe not because a chief cook was missing.'

Come, on, then, what did you create that was so special?' Tommy asked, grinning, probably thinking he was winding Hamish up.

'Do you have a girlfriend at home?' Hamish asked.

'No,' Tommy replied, looking away shyly.

'You a hump and dump practitioner, then?' Hamish asked.

'A what?' Tommy erupted, his pot stirring briefly ceasing.

'Do you practice a catch and release strategy?' Hamish continued his questioning.

'That's something else I know nothing about,' Tommy said, 'you can feck off.'

'You must find wanking a well of humorous possibilities, then?'

'Feck off! You're good at making mince. You can create nothing special. Answer me that?'

Tommy was being cheeky. Hamish thought he'd continue take the piss.

'Special, you ask. Working with vegetable oil technicians and dietary innovators from the Indian Sub-continent, I created the slipperiest cooking oil known to man.'

'What was that?, Tommy asked, moving to another pot and stirring. Hamish was drawing him in.

'The mix of cooking oils, both exotic and expensive, others spicy, was my secret. I gave it an emotive name and registered the patent as S.L.U.R.R.R.P, all capital letters. You had to roll your Rs to sound it right. It revolutionised the curry house cooks, takeaway businesses and ship's cook preparation of curies. It made the hottest curry in the world, the phaal, the vindaloo, and other spicy dishes, down to a korma, pleasant, edible and colon passing experience for humans. Stir that mince again. If it catches on the bottom of the pan, we'll have fewer portions to serve up.

'The diner, in any eatery, selecting from the menu any curry dish the chef created using s,l,u,r,r,r,p, will find that the slickly greased stool aftermath speedily navigates the anal canal, exits the ringpiece at hypersonic speed, soundlessly, leaving it cool with no trace of the excretion adhering to its periphery.'

'Feck, s,l,u,r,r,r,p, Tommy spluttered, 'a shite like nothing on earth, going through the sound barrier without the bang, amazing,' he erupted, wiping his forehead with a tea towel.

'This oil created a non-wipe, pain-free passing. It became a catering industry standard,' continued Hamish. He smiled, noticing Tommy wiping sweat away. 'Curry chefs became renowned for their creations, and curry hounds repeatedly used their favourite takeaways and curry house, had curries for breakfast, lunch and dinner seven days a week, pleased that the chef used s,l,u,r,r,r,p in their creations. I'll see if I can order a supply for use on here.'

'What will that benefit us working on here?' Tommy asked.

'For *you* it means you'll not find skidmarks 8 inch long soiling your underpants.'

Hamish eyed Tommy, wondered if he'd bought the story, watched him thinking, his eyes looking up into his head. 'Don't let the mince stick to the bottom of that pan,' he instructed, 'I won't be long away.'

Gards were knocking on crew accommodation doors as Hamish walked along the Port alleyway towards the crew deck. Stepping over the coaming, he saw that the only top deck freight was unaccompanied flat trailers without any loads and a farmer's cattle trailer carrying goats that were looking through the gaps and sounding off a succession of bleats. He walked down the stairs and then along the Port side of the deck, taking in the view towards the town. He clicked on Jennie's tag on the mobile. Her phone rang. She answered quickly, 'Are you safe?' she asked. 'I saw on the news that a cook was missing from a ferry running to the republic.'

'Just thought I'd give you a call so you could hear my voice and know that I'm well. Aye, it's true about Flick Fleck the chief cook. I'm run off my feet here, doing the job of two.'

'That will always be hard for the workshy, but I wouldn't want ever to tell the twins that daddy is missing.'

'It wouldn't bother you, though?'

'It might not have done in the past, but you've settled down, grown up, become more mature. You just about get a pass mark in my book, apart from the state of your underwear. I've told you often enough to wipe your arse properly.'

'Thanks for that. It's been an interesting three days. I'm sure we'll have another cook onboard in a day or two. I'll get by. I'll bring my soiled washing home for you to launder. Won't have time to do it on here. I'll have to rush. Almost time to feed the masses. They're always hungry. Bye.'

At the stern, Hamish looked over at the loading ramp and saw crew had fully raised it, loading completed. Looking over the ship starboard side as he heard the rumble of the main engines starting up, he noticed the Gardai launch nudging away from the ship side, a uniformed Gard in the cabin at the wheel.

A brief glance towards the forward end of the ship the package hanging from a porthole caught his eye. He thought it must be Tara and Cara's cabin. Funny way to dry their bras, his take on the shape and size of the package. Thinking he'd been out in the fresh long enough, he entered the crew accommodation and ambled along the starboard alleyway, stopping briefly and listening to music coming through door grills. Tara was coming out of her shared cabin, kitted out to start work. He said to her, letting out a short titter as he said it, 'Better get your bras in from the porthole otherwise the Gards in that launch next to the ferry will want to know why you've parachutes hanging out to dry.'

'Shite,' Tara said, her face grimacing, plainly unhappy at what Hamish said. Throwing her forehead higher she turned, took a long stride back into the cabin, and slammed the door shut, without eyeing him up and down, without a suggestive twinkle in her eye, like she had on the occasions she'd passed by or sat next to him.

'Glad to be of service,' Hamish said towards the door grill, but no one else was within earshot to hear him.

Chapter 34

Back in the office following his galley visit, Rupert sat musing, mobile in hand, considering the best time to call home, thinking back to previous Saturday scrabble commitments his wife might have had. Passenger numbers had not increased this unscheduled docking in Ballymagilligan, the three already onboard were taking turns playing the puggy. A crash of coins rattling the winnings receptacle and a loud cheer raised his head to look through the grill towards the three. He was about to dial his home number when an Irish voice through the grill asked, 'Can you change a hundred quid's worth of pound coins for Euro notes? We've just won a jackpot.'

It took him five minutes to check the exchange rate, count out five piles of twenty coins, hand over the equivalent notes and a handful of coins that allowed an easily divisible by three winning Euro amount.

That chore over, the cash box back in the safe and he reseated, a Gard lowered his head and stuck it through the hatch and said, 'Your turn with the commander, Mr Sewell, has arrived. Come with me.'

In the smokeroom, the commander ushered Rupert into the facing chair. 'You know why you're here. We're interviewing all crew in an effort to understand what happened to Mr Fleck, your cook. Do you know anything of interest?'

'Absolutely nothing. Mr Fleck came to see me yesterday, told me he wanted to resign, pay off next Wednesday, as he had a job ashore working as a chef in your local Gardai station canteen. He seemed happy that he had the job, his wife being wheelchair bound and receiving care from family and care workers whilst he was at sea. It seems highly unlikely to me that he would have taken his own life. I thought he was taking the less worrying choice for both him and his family.'

'We've just listened to Mr drake the bosun's story. I deduced, from what he told us, he doesn't seem to be a fan of yours or any officer. He has suggested that you might have ambushed Mr Fleck on the after deck, chinned him about the misuse of steaks, pushed him whilst he was in an unsteady state, under the influence of drink, and he toppled over the side. What have you to say about that?'

Hearing those words, Rupert's face and neck had turned florid. He was seething. Severely irked. He threw his shoulders back, tightened his lips to thin strips of pink and said, 'I rarely swear but that scouse bastard said that, did he. I was nowhere near the after deck. Have never, in the four days I've been purser on here, put a foot on that deck.

'If I have the time of Mr Fleck's disappearance correct, I was in bed, asleep, until I had a shocking experience that awakened me in the early hours, on feeling the rough tongue of a goat that I found in my bedroom, licking my face. We carried a trailer load of goats that crossing. They must be still onboard now. In my shocked state I must have knocked my bedside clock from the cabinet. I put my reading light on, found it and retrieved it but couldn't find the battery or the cover. Still haven't found the battery or the cover. The goat might have eaten the damned things. The clock will have stopped at the precise time the battery shot from its housing. The clock you will find in my cabin. Check what I'm saying. And the bridge officer will confirm where I was when I rang up and asked for someone to remove the beast before it shit all over my bedroom floor.

'I've heard grumbles and silliness from Mr Drake. He's supposed to be the crew rep. A crewmember locked me into the ferry cold stores, from which Tommy the galley boy freed me when I pushed the alarm plunger. I've had a loud, annoying raspberry blown down my telephone. I've tore apart a bread roll at dinner to find what looked like a nasal extraction in the centre. The experience nearly had me spewing, it did. Jokers are employed on this ship and are disgruntled by the management's steak only on a Sunday decision.

'When you find the criminals who tried to end Mr Fleck's life, perhaps the silliness will disappear when you arrest them and remove them from the ferry. I hope you find them soon.'

'Relax,' Dunlevy said, seeing that his words had upset Rupert to a degree he hadn't expected, 'neither I nor Inspector Power believed a word that Drake spouted. I can tell you this now, but you must keep it under your hat until I announce otherwise, but Mr Fleck is safe but under observation. He might not be as well as he once was, but he's tucked up in bed at the local cottage hospital. A monk from the Priory on Lobhar Island pulled him alive from the water. He's an incredibly lucky man. He said two men who didn't speak held him over the ship's side by his legs and trouser belt. He slipped out of his loosely fitting cook's trousers and galley footwear and fell into the sea. He also has what might be a stab wound, certainly a cut to his side. The light of a buoy attracted him. He doggy paddled to the buoy and clung on. Doesn't know how long he was clinging to it. That's where the monk found him. The monks resident at the Priory did a good job warming him up, got his blood flowing. Rescue services helicoptered him out.'

'I cannot point a finger because I don't know what happened to Mr

Fleck,' Rupert began, 'company management asked me to make changes in crew feeding. They also asked me to advise on ways to stop crew thieving onboard. I know that the personnel manager, who is onboard, told Mr Fleck that steaks will now be a choice only on a Sunday dinner, not a choice every day.

'In your experience, is it common to find jokers onboard merchant ships,' Dunlevy asked.

'No, no, I didn't mean it like that. Ship's crews are usually a mixture of experienced deck, engine room and catering ratings and first trippers in those departments. But boredom can set in quickly on ships. Crew, finding little to entertain them, start taking the piss out of each other. That should not ever be the case on this ferry that's in port thrice a day with tv sets that work in port. The crew are not three weeks at sea crossing oceans, between ports, with nothing but short wave radio to tune into. I think the problem on here is a combination of jokers, and more sinister elements trying to keep the status quo of steaks on the menu for dinner every day and more to thieve, to take home on trip off day to feed the family. If I find other thieving in the bar and cafeteria I have to report it and find ways to end it. I'm sure if security checked all passenger and crew personal luggage when they left the ferry they'd have more arrests. Certain crew elements will not fondly respect me on here. It's an irksome challenge that I have, and I won't be Mr Popular if the company change to an accountable way of running the crew feeding, cafeteria and bar services.'

Dunlevy was checking the crew list as he said to Rupert, 'You can go now. I don't think I'll need to speak to you again.'

*Rupert had only a minute to look round his office when the gong sounded announcing lunch. He locked up and sauntered into the saloon, checking his uniform and tie position as he went. He chose to sit in the usual chair and waited for Cara to present him with a menu, and the arrival of other officers.

He could tell that Bo cleaned up easily: he was the first to arrive, didn't look sweaty, and claimed the chair opposite Rupert, who was sure Bo had let out a barely audible baa as he sat down. He wasn't going to rise to that bait, preferring to let sleeping goats lie. Screwfix arrived next and took the chair next to Bo. He didn't look sweaty either. Lamping up wasn't an arduous task were his recollections of what ships engineers thought was ship's electricians main task.

Cara placed two menus on the table. Bo grabbed one. He was quickly outraged, mouthing, 'Suffering fuck are we down to mince and tatties on here, but?' Screwfix shook his head, and said, 'We're lucky to have this as a menu choice. The galley a man short, the staff called away to search for Flick and for Gardai grilling, what did you expect, but?'

'I'm pleased someone sees sense on here,' Rupert said, glaring at Bo, 'it's enough hearing untruthful crowd complaints about the feeding when we're fully manned.'

The table filled. It pleased Rupert that the other officers didn't 'rip the piss' out of the hastily devised menu and no one mouthed a baa to rile him further. He said, 'I'm hoping dinner tonight will be to your liking. I'm sure Hamish will have roasts readied for the oven. Steaks tomorrow night, by the way. I'll have a word with the Personnel Officer whilst she's on board to get another cook employed quickly. Sought after jobs shouldn't be difficult to fill.'

'At least the mince is tastiest I've had on here. Must have been the extra oxo,' Bo said, then the table quietened whilst they ate.

Rupert thought better than to remark on Bo's taste bud test but changed his mind as he looked at the menu and mentioned, thinking it would create a laugh, 'I was worried about horse meat in supermarket ready meals away back in 1959 when the wonderfully named bay gelding horse Oxo won the Aintree grand national.'

'I hope any of its offcuts didn't find their way into the mince pot on here,' Bo shot back to laughs from all except Rupert, doing his damnedest not to look irked.

Captain Davies entered the saloon and pulled out chairs at his table for Abi, Commander Dunlevy and Inspector Power to take, leaving just enough room for the chief engineer and chief officer to squeeze in.

'How are your engines doing,' the captain asked the chief engineer.

'We're doing all the revs we can,' the chief's stock reply, 'the repairs were all good.'

*Cara felt her body chill as she saw Dunlevy enter the saloon. She thought his face arrogant and holier than thou. She and Tara swore they'd would never forget it. Her mind flew back to their mother's court case. Along with Paddy, their father, and two sets of grandparents, they had listened to Dunlevy, then the Gardai inspector responsible in the District Court for prosecuting offenders of non-serious crimes, like common up to serious assaults, describe her mother Dolores as a wanton slut who deserved a prison sentence. He had failed to mention or summon witnesses to attest to the fact that the assaulted woman had begun the altercation, suggesting loudly, so the entire pub crowd to hear, that Dolly was 'on the game' and a common tart, which was a nasty twisting of the truth, a downright lie.

Cara served the captain's table guest with her usual good grace. Tara would be interested to know Dunlevy was onboard. She would tell her later.

Chapter 35

Tara had waited until she heard the engines speeding up as the ferry steamed out of the buoyed channel into deeper water. She had knifed holes in the sealed package and the inflatable device. Secreting the package, trapping it under her jacket, high in an oxter between arm and chest, she left the cabin, checked the alleyway was clear, opened the door to the top freight deck, stepped over the coaming and begun her walk towards the stern. As well as she could, she kept the trailers between her and the accommodation. Dark smoke shot in pulses from the funnel but blew away, not doing anything to shield her movements. She hoped no one would spot her activities or wonder what she was doing on the deck.

She reached the stern, stepped around coiled mooring ropes and a capstan winch, the stern rail was right ahead. At the side of the stern door she looked over the rail to the churning wash created by the twin propellors. She thought the wash would easily consume the package. She raised the concealing arm. She passed it over the rail in a quick, single movement. The package released she felt it slide down her side without snagging then watched it drop into the ferry's foaming wake. She saw no trace of it on the surface as the ferry sailed on. That Davy Jones had taken it to his locker crossed her mind, the contents might make him more agreeable to doomed sailors.

Pleased that the ditched package had disappeared without trace, she'd have to tell Cara what she knew and had done to keep them out of the Gardai's mitts. Later, a more awkward moment might rear its ugly head when she or Cara told their father that they had to abort the mission and why. But dad would understand, wouldn't want his daughters arrested for their part in drug running, at any time, or now whilst Gardai were onboard, and the package leading them back to him. She blessed Hamish for noticing the package and passing word of the police launch, even if his description was a mile of silk out; a feckin parachute: who was he feckin kidding! Cara would like that. She would shag him as a reward if Cara didn't get him first.

*Rupert, to show no disappointment at the menu went through it from soup, entrée, main course and sweet. He noted all at the table had devoured the fare without any further complaint. He ordered a coffee which he lifted and took with him when he left the table. Passing the captain's table Abi lifted her head and said to him, 'I'll see you in the office when I've finished lunch.'

*'I cannot remember when I last had mince and tatties for lunch but

what Hamish cooked up was delicious,' Abi said as she walked through the office door half an hour later.

Rupert had sat composing a text to send to his wife. He thought he should as he didn't know how busy he might be in Holyhead to make a call and he still hadn't remembered what her scrabble schedule might be. He stood up, fetched the spare chair from his bedroom and placed it in front of the desk at what he thought was a safe-from-molestation distance from an exploring hand.

'Dunlevy has already told you of Mr Fleck's rescue,' Abi said as she sat down, made herself comfortable..

'Surely must be a miracle to survive such an ordeal,' Rupert said.

Abi spoke softly, lifting her head to look through the office hatch to make sure the foyer was free of eavesdroppers, 'Dunlevy hasn't named any culprits yet but he's having Higson in right after lunch. He says that he will first assess Higson's demeanour, look for signs of nervousness and hit him hard; with accusations of attempted murder, or even murder, I suppose, though he says he has something up his sleeve that the Gards found on their cabin search. He didn't reveal what. If Higson admits that he and the bosun were responsible, It means their removal under arrest from the ferry. I'll feel relieved that other crew might feel safer and we can get back to running a ferry service of which we can be proud.'

'It sure has been an interesting three days, unlike any during my deep sea career,' Rupert said.

'I've ordered the 25 mil bar optic spirit measures with counter. They should arrive before you take your trip off. I'm hoping they do the trick and we can introduce them without hassle, and accusations from the bar staff that we don't trust them. Once the optics are in use, you can tell them it's to match with a new online ordering system we're introducing.'

Rupert didn't answer but thought he wouldn't be taking a late night stroll along the top deck anytime soon.

'When the new optics arrive, which I hope will be next week,' Abi said, deep in thought, 'I'll do another crossing, fit the optics myself. I'll make ensure the bar staff know that it's a company policy and not one you have dreamed up. That should settle your mind. Not tempt bar staff to threaten you. I'll run past Fred whether we should have notices printed to warn passengers to only accept spirits from a measured optic and to check the price the barperson rings up.'

'I could have fitted them ok, but you're correct, Rupert said, 'that it's company policy will remove the onus from me. I'm hoping we have another cook onboard early next week. Hamish is coping admirably under pressure. You could promote him to chief cook and Tommy up to second cook if you cannot find a replacement chief cook. Tommy has worked the galley for almost two years, I see from his discharge book. He should have enough knowledge and experience by now. I'll have a word with Hamish to see if that is acceptable to him and let you know before you leave us in Holyhead.'

Abi had listened closely to Rupert. Hamish's tenure on the ferry was finite. He'd be back to policing next week or the week after, depending on his commander generosity. She'd have to explain to Rupert Hamish's presence onboard as well as the need for an experienced cook. 'What I'm about to tell you Rupert, what we were eventually going to make you aware of is that Hamish is an undercover cop from London's Met police. He's here to suss out if crooks are using the ferry for drug and people trafficking. It's hush hush, as you would imagine. Only the captain and now you know of this arrangement. You'll have to keep it that way. I don't yet know if he has found anything of significance.

'He was also supposed to be looking into crew thieving, bar fiddles and steak theft. If he discovers anything, no doubt he'll inform the Garda or Holyhead police through his Met commander, when he has any evidence. He hasn't had the time onboard to tackle anything but galley work.

'You have alerted me to a method a barperson can fiddle a bar transactions. We will sort that out with the new optics. The overuse of steaks I have sorted out, displeasing crewmembers as we have found out. You'll have to tell your second steward to keep a check on the steak numbers we have in stock. The new tills should tell us if the numbers coming onboard equate to normal usage, sales and crew feeding. I take it you are still keen to continue your days at sea with us, Rupert?' Abi picked up her handbag and made to leave, 'I'll go and collect my things ready to go ashore, but I'll be back onboard to do another round trip quite soon.'

Rupert stood, up, said, 'To be sure, excuse my Irishism, but I'm sure the ferry will settle down to a normal routine, and we'll all be happier for it.

Abi winked at Rupert and left the office, eying him wickedly over a shoulder.

*On leaving the saloon, Dunlevy thanked Captain Davies and Abi for providing a grand lunch, and suggested beef mince with colcannon that would make an enjoyable difference to the plain, old spud. A Gard approached as they chatted and ushered Dunlevy to one side. The Gard told him the inspector, who'd been on standby at the cottage hospital, wanted a word. On the bridge, the officer on watch familiarised Dunlevy with the radio telephone system, how to make the call personal and put him through.

Back in the officer's smoke room, Dunlevy said to Inspector Power, 'Let's get Gards to bring Higson up here. I have just learned something that might make him feel extremely worried. You go with the Gards. In his cabin, retrieve the belt without the buckle searchers reported they found in his donkey jacket pocket. I've just learned Mr Fleck can recall his belt giving way, that the buckle was never the securest of attachments, maybe he left it unfastened as he had recently been to the toilet. Perhaps, if the belt came adrift in Higson's hand, and without thinking too well, he rolled up the belt around his knuckles, placed it in his donkey jacket pocket, either absentmindedly or with theft in mind. Rolled up to fit into the pocket was the way searchers found it. He remembered something else as well that will get the pair of them.

'I'll begin by buttering him up. Tell him he was a man ever thoughtful of saving life at sea and deserves a medal for throwing the lifejacket after Mr Fleck, as he dropped into the sea. I'll see how he bites. He might break down quickly and relate to me the entire saga, blaming Drake for involving him. If he's belligerent, I'll have him turn his pockets out. If we're lucky, he'll have the missing buckle amongst his small change. If he has, and we can match the buckle up to the belt, we'll have him. But I'll let him stew. Mr Fleck said he had burned his name, Sean Fleck, with a hot electric soldering iron, onto the inside of the leather belt. I'll check that out. If the name is where he says it is, Higson's done for. As guilty as hell. Mr Fleck recognizing the belt as his should convince a jury of his guilt.'

Dunlevy thought Ted Higson was walking on his heels as loud throaty grunts erupted from his wide-open mouth, apprehension noticeable, as the Gard at each side of him pushed him into the Officer's Lounge. Dunlevy said nothing but raised an arm and pointed Ted towards the chair facing him. He spoke the Judges Rule and then began the interview. 'Ted, we're recording this interview. You don't look much of a hero, Ted, but I'm sure you are,' was his first comment. Ted made no reply, his eyes looking towards the deckhead, his hands in working gloves he clapped together.

'Mr Drake didn't tell me otherwise when we interviewed him, but it was you who threw the lifebelt after Mr Fleck when he went overboard, wasn't it,' he rattled off quickly, watching Ted closely for any reaction. Ted didn't react, his eyes scanning the wall posters and elsewhere, anywhere than towards Dunlevy.

'If it were you, it could get you off a murder charge, Ted,' Dunlevy offered, his smile a false gesture of friendship as Ted finally looked towards him.

Ted erupted, 'I don't know what Dick Drake told you, but have you found a body?' his eyes on Dunlevy.

'We will reveal that shortly, but someone threw a lifebelt to Mr Fleck. We've found the lifebelt and we know it came from this ferry. I'll ask you again. It was you who threw the lifebelt to Mr Fleck when he went overboard wasn't it?' Ted said nothing, retrained his eyes towards the deckhead.

Inspector Power knocked and entered the lounge, the belt hidden behind his back.

'Ted, would you stand up, please?' Dunlevy asked. 'Ted, would you please turn your pockets out onto the table.' Dunlevy moved a table between him and Ted.

Ted removed his gloves, threw them behind him onto the chair, and uttered, 'What the fuck has this got to do with me.' He stuck a hand in each jean pocket and placed on the table coins, a piece of string, and a five Euro note that hid, until Dunlevy moved it, a belt buckle with a twisted securing pin, onto the table.

'Is that everything, Ted, your back pockets, too.'

'Aye, that's your lot. Can I go now? You can stick that small change into a charity box.' Ted said. A look of annoyance on his face he made a sweeping hand gesture, thumb raised pointing towards Dunlevy then the door.

'No, you can sit down now. We haven't finished with you yet, Dunlevy spat out at him.'

Inspector Power stepped forward, placed the coiled belt on the table. Dunlevy unwound it, sought out the buckle end, picked up the buckle, held it to the belt and said, 'I think we can match up the buckle and belt with the one Mr Fleck was wearing when you and Drake grabbed him and threw him overboard, Ted. What have you to say to that?'

'I threw the lifebelt after Flick,' Ted shouted out, as if he couldn't get the words out quick enough. 'It wasn't my idea to scare the shit out of him, get steaks back on the menu. It was Dick's idea.

'In Dick, do you mean Mr Drake the bosun?'

'Aye. I wasn't keen but he said it would work. I went along with the scare. It went horribly wrong. Flick's belt came away in my hands. I don't know what made me put the belt in my pocket. The buckle came off as I was doing it. We never intended him any harm. It was supposed to scare the shit out of him, start and finish.'

To Inspector Power, Dunlevy said, 'Take Gards with you and Arrest Mr Drake. Read him his rights and fetch him here. Before that, take Mr Higson and place him securely in the van. To Ted, he said, 'You are a lucky man. A monk pulled Mr Fleck out of the sea in the early hours of this morning. He is safe and recovering in hospital. We will charge you, when we get you back to the republic, of endangering his life. It could have been a murder or manslaughter charge. You will have to hope that he recovers fully.'

'You won't find Dick onboard,' Ted said, wringing his hands, looking away.

'You what?' Dunlevy erupted, 'explain, man.'

'While you were at lunch, about ten minutes before you dragged me up here, I had my ear on a tumbler placed on the bulkhead between my cabin and Dick's. I hear voices. I heard him say he was going to give evidence that it was me, and me alone, who held Flick over the side and that he tried to stop me. I waited for his chat partner to leave his cabin. I knocked on his cabin door. Told him I wanted to run something past him, outside on our deck. I took him by the arm and led him towards the rail, saying, "I think we should have a word about what we agreed." I took a run at him and sent him flying over the rails. I hope the bastard dies. He always thought me soft in the fucking head, someone he could push around, but I got him for it. You can charge me with that too.'

Dunlevy turned to Inspector Power, 'Quick as you can, before you go and check if Drake is or isn't in his cabin, send a Gard up to the bridge to report we could have another man overboard in the sea situation. The captain won't be happy that he has to turn the ferry around again. But he'll have to.'

Suddenly, Ted swivelled his backside in his chair and erupted, his eyes steady on Dunlevy's face. 'I think you should hang about, hear what I've to say. I've been taking the piss. You'll find Dick Drake asleep in his cabin. We had nothing to do with Flick going over the side. That belt is mine. I've had it since my first trip to sea. I've put extra holes in it so it goes round my guts. I still have the receipt from the Rawhide leather shop back in Liverpool. It's in my cabin. You'll have to fabricate something better than a belt to stitch us up with. Thought I was a dafty, did you, couldn't make up a story to fool you lot of thick Paddies.'

'Ag cur an phiss, as we say in Irish, taking the piss, you say,' Dunlevy shot back, his face changing from untroubled to one of contempt. 'We have other evidence to link you pair to this crime. Don't count your chickens too soon or look forward to a steak on Sunday. Inspector, search him thoroughly, take him down to the van and lock him up. Then, check the claim the Mr Drake is having forty winks. Leave four Gards with him in his cabin. Only let him out for toilet needs but under escort. If not, we'll have to see the captain. If we have two prisoners to take back to the republic I'll ask for the helicopter to land onboard whilst the ferry is alongside in Holyhead and get them off quickly. You and three Gards can escort them.'

Dunlevy gave himself a pat on the shoulders when he saw the name Sean Fleck burned onto the inside of the leather belt. 'It's yours, Sean Fleck,' he said to himself, as Inspector Power closed the door behind him, 'a feckin belter, and if I'm not mistaken a Stanley knife could have made that cut in the belt. One of them cut the belt to make sure the cook did fall into the sea and drown.'

Chapter 36

Five minutes after Inspector Power left the officer's lounge, Commander Dunlevy had two prisoners. Dick Drake was alive, well, but soon not to be a happy Scouser. Laid on his side, in his working gear, he was snoring with irregular resonant clamour when Inspector Power strode into his smoky cabin without knocking, accompanied by four Gards.

Power told Drake, as he turned and lifted his head from the pillow, 'Wake up Drake, you're under arrest and being charged along with Higson, for the attempted murder of Sean Fleck.'

Gards snapped handcuffs on Drake, who spat out, guessing Ted had fucked up, 'Fucking daft bastard gave the game away.' Each Gard had a hard to hide smile on their face.

They sat Drake on his bunk. The inspector recited Drake his rights.

'How did that daft fucker give the game away,' Drake bawled.

'He had the cooks trouser belt in his duffle coat pocket. The belt had the cook's name burned into the inside of it. Like a brand, it's proof of ownership. Proof enough of you pair being involved. The good news, what nobody has told you yet, is that the cook is alive and recovering, in the cottage hospital back in Ballymagilligan. You must sincerely hope he does not relapse and die from the effects of your assault and cold water immersion. You'll answer the charge on Monday in the Republic.'

The inspector picked up the bosun's belt that held his splicing spike and Stanley knife and left the cabin to tell Dunlevy how things went. Gards moved the cabin chair to the closed door. A Gard sat on it blocking escape. The other three sat on his day bed, waiting further orders. watching an unhappy man resting his head in his hands, literally.

*Captain Davies was on the bridge when Dunlevy found him. 'Docking might take a little longer,' the captain told Dunlevy. 'We have to wait a free berth becoming available as we're away out of schedule and other ferry companies use them. I would not expect them to give up a berth for us. Harbour control have just told me that we cannot get alongside until at least16:00 hours. We have to get alongside, discharge, then we have a full load going back. The manifest says we have road trains to load, that's an articulate pulling a trailer if you're unfamiliar with them. The reversing of those down the ramp and into line on the lower deck will take time. A normal full load takes two hours to load. But so long as the remaining seamen don't go on strike, and the chief engineer has the engines in good order, we will manage it in time for the crew to take a Saturday night pint in the local at Ballymagilligan before the pub shut,' he said cheerily.

At anchor just off the Holyhead Harbour breakwater the captain, chief officer, second mate and quartermaster watched as a Stenna Line ferry left the harbour and headed on its course for Dublin. 16:00 hours had passed. Seamen had already raised the anchor and the captain had ordered, 'Ring Stand By in the engine room.' When the engine room answered, he ordered, 'Half ahead both engines, start bow thruster, and have what's left of the deck crowd go to their stations.' The watchkeeping second mate, stood nearby, in the bridge house, his ears tuned for the captain's next orders on the bridge to engine room telegraph.

'I've used my mobile to contact Dublin,' Dunlevy told the captain as they stood together on the starboard bridge wing, 'a Gardai helicopter will arrive within the hour to take the prisoners back to Pearse Street Garda Station in Dublin. I'll process them when I return. They'll be up in front of the beak on Monday. The whirlybird should be on its way now. The pilot will need permission to land on your top deck if that's ok with you. If you haven't completely cleared the top deck the chopper will circle until it's all clear to land. Getting them onto the craft and strapped in, along with Inspector Power and the Gards travelling with them, shouldn't take long or disrupt loading.'

Log 2 of Hamish Macnab.

Before joining the Holigan Express it occurred to me that working on a ferry had to be no different to working on a deep sea ship. The personnel needed were the same. The engine room department oversaw the smooth running of the main engines and auxiliaries and maintained them in good working order. The navigators, or fruitbats, as they were known in my day, the nickname originating from the observation, rightly or wrongly perceived, that they hung about and did nothing; whilst all they did was to plot the courses and for the vessel to reach each port safely. Ferry navigators also loaded the lorries and other vehicles onto decks, ensuring they were shackled down and not likely to break loose during a crossing. Deck ratings tied the ferry up to the quay at each docking. The catering department of galley staff fed all ranks and passengers. Stewards served food to passengers and officers and cleaned officer accommodation.

How wrong was I?

The main difference is that the ferry is in the same port twice a day, not like a real ship, weeks out on the oggin between ports, crossing oceans to reach the next one, shipping cargo around the World. Ferry crew and officers work one week on for one week off with pay. All crew can take earned annual leave, with pay, and take it regularly.

What did I find?

Crewmembers were unhappy. Why, when pay and leave were exceptional? Why did crew steal food to take home when going on leave? Why was suspicion lurking that the passenger bar staff were placing their own spirit bottles on optic, selling the measures and pocketing the money?

That the thieves onboard Holigan Express were a shower of greedy bastards often crossed my mind. Felons had existed since recorded time, certainly since the time of the well-documented thief Barabbas; all races had their pirates, bandits, thieves, hucksters, snake oil salesmen and petty crooks.

And then we had the mystery of the missing Chief Cook Sean Fleck. It turned out not to be a mystery but an attempt by two crew members to coerce him into continuing to allow steaks as a menu choice for lunch and dinner and the grand steak larceny, purloining of the sirloin by crewmembers. Tossing him overboard, nearly costing him his life, in the early hours of a morning, whilst the ferry was leaving the port of Ballymagilligan for the port of Holyhead. How serious, malicious, unthought-through an act was that?

As I write, news of the chief cook's miraculous rescue had reached me and that he is safe, being nursed back to health in the cottage hospital of the Irish port. I doubt he will return to the work on the ferry. He had already handed in his notice to quit and has a job to go to as chef in a Gardai canteen. It was his intention to pack in seagoing employment and take the job ashore for personal reasons. Later, the news that the Gardai had arrested the seamen Drake and Higson reached me. These two seamen had announced their troublemaking qualities when idiotically complaining that we were feeding them horse meat. Gardai have scheduled a helicopter to uplift them in the port of Holyhead to take them back for formal charging and to trial in the Republic. I hope they get what they deserve.

Since the disappearance of the chief cook, you should readily believe that I have been too busy cooking for snooping. A man down in the galley has increased the workload on both me and the galley boy, who is able, a bit naive, but deserves a leg up in status to the rank of second cook, when the company appoint a replacement chief cook. I have no intention of applying for the position of chief cook, though I have the qualifications and culinary talents for the job.

However, as I reported to Commander Dunlevy I recommended a look at a transit van that I thought had dogs locked up in the back and might be heading for an illegal puppy farm in the republic. I'll not need to look out for it if it returns to the UK. The Gardai found a large quantity of cocaine in the dog bed, arrests were made. I haven't had the opportunity to look at lorries crossing on the main deck for instances of people smuggling. I have visited the main deck whilst the ferry was underway. The noise of the engines, the vibration, the banging and the rattling of the shackles securing the lorries to the deck was excessive. Refrigerated lorries kicked out noise, even after the ship's electrician had connected those lorry's refrigeration plant to the ferry's electric supply for the crossing.

And as for hearing voices; shouts or screams for help from the interior of locked and sealed articulated lorry box or refrigerated waggon would be impossible.

And as for drugs; I've smelt no instances of crew or passengers smoking cannabis on board nor have I heard of any chat about drugs. When I am in their vicinity Irish crewmembers tend to converse with each other in Gaelic which I do not understand.

Chapter 37

Saturday afternoon, soon after docking in Holyhead, Hamish put the galley out of bounds to visitors. The ferry had never had an overnight stay in Ballymagilligan before and crewmembers were badgering Tommy for a list good-night-ashore venues, night spots and pubs where a fanny hunter might be lucky in love, or luckier, without having to promise love ever after. Hamish wasn't all that interested but might try a Guinness in the pub outside the dock gates. The dinner roast was honey-mustard glazed ham, the crackling had crisped nicely, the joints cooked and resting. The peas pudding he had made to his own recipe.

Abi had said her goodbyes to Rupert and rushed off the ferry with the three passengers. Fred waited on the quay in a taxi to take her home.

Rupert heard the gong sound for dinner before he heard the racket the helicopter was kicking out as it circled to land on the top deck. He didn't bother to venture out on deck to view the proceedings.

'We won't sail before six. I noticed on the dockside a bunch of accompanied lorries and road trains. They always take more time to reverse down the ramp and into position than a trailer driven by an experienced docker.' Bo said as Rubert took the seat facing him at the saloon table, 'I'll be on standby but I should have time to eat dinner before I've to go down the engine room again. But I'll be ashore tonight for a pint or two. You fancy coming along, Rupert. I've had the lowdown on the good Saturday night spots. Fanny in abundance, I'm told and all game for it. What do you think?'

'I'm not desperate,' Rupert responded, wondering when that might be true, 'I've only been away from home 3 days. Surely you can go a week without getting your end away?'

'I'm single, and unless I'm working I'll always take the opportunity to go ashore. On this old tub you never know when the chief will turn engineers to, to do a job. It should be good fun, new surroundings and tasty colleens to cast my eyes over, but. Looking forward to the run ashore, aren't we boys,' Bo said, pointing down the table to Toots and Screwfix who had joined them.

The captain walked into the saloon with Commander Dunlevy, the commander taking a chair at his table. The captain made a beeline for the junior officer's table. Both Toots and Screwfix were smiling and nodding their heads as the captain approached. 'Sorry to disappoint you boys but I have had orders to return empty to Holyhead tonight and anchor out until we berth on Sunday night to start loading for tomorrow's overnight run on schedule. You'll have time to go to the Gilligan pub but don't be late back. I'll announce shore leave to end at 12:30 a.m. Will be sailing soon after. Don't be late back. Anyone missing the ship should know their name will be in the logbook and will lose a day's pay, maybe their job. I'm sure you all know the score but I'm not so sure about the crew.' The captain shrugged his shoulders, turned and took his seat at his table.

With the smile wiped from his face Bo said, 'That's that idea well and truly fucked. The chief had no important jobs scheduled whilst we were alongside We'd have had a good run ashore. Us engineers must be doing too good a job down in the hole. The chief never comes down to see what's going on. He's always on the end of the telephone. His knees must be too wonky for him to take to the staircase. He might get down to the control platform but doubt if he'd get back up again. He could only have damaged his knees walking from his cabin to the bar, but I'm too shit scared to mention that to him.'

Toots and Screwfix let out a shrieks of laughter.

Chapter 38

Cara was waiting in the cabin as Tara returned from her dumping overboard of the drug cache. 'It's done,' she said, 'it's over the side, sinking into the depths. I watched it disappear. The Gardai cannot do us now for a drug find. I'm sure you will, and dad will, agree it was the correct move with Gardai onboard.

'You're quite right,' replied Cara, 'but listen to this. The Gard commander in charge of the squad on here is no other than that bastard Dunlevy who put our mother away for the three month stretch. He's been in the saloon with the captain. I came over quite cold on seeing that cruel, smug, sanctimonious face of the bastard again.'

'You're feckin joking, having me on?' Tara said as she fiddled with her bra and turned to face Cara.

'No. It's him alright. You'll know when you see him.' Cara could tell Tara was deep in thought when she asked her, 'You're not thinking of doing anything silly, are you?'

'Would I?' Tara replied.

'If I know you, yes,' Cara said louder than in her usual voice.

'Now that he's arrested and helicoptered Dick and Ted back to Dublin, I wonder if he's still interviewing crew? I'd like to hear what he has to say,' Tara replied.

*Head Pathologist Darcy O'Darragh had returned to his duties at Dublin City mortuary on the first Monday of the new year. He'd been off work for a two week sabbatical since before Christmas, visiting relatives settled and living the good life on Long Island in the United States.

Full of energy and motivated he checked the details of any cases passing through the mortuary whilst he was away. He was astonished to find that the body of Hugh Rice was still occupying a shelf in the refrigerated unit and that no one had claimed it. Perhaps it was the festive season holidays that had caused the delayed uplift by undertakers for burial or cremation. Concerned that the paperwork was correct, he pulled the shelf from the unit and opened the bodybag to check it still held the body of Hugh Rice.

It was Hugh Rice he saw but what attracted his attention wasn't Hugh's bleak dead face but the small chunk of chewing gum that sat directly beneath an ear. How could he and his staff have missed it, who could have inserted it in the aural cavity, when did that happen and under what circumstances, his thoughts. Perhaps his and his assistants rush before the holidays had led to slapdash practices and they had not looked past the earlobes. He concluded that the gum must have shrank in the chill of the refrigerator, the vibration of an adjacent unit opening and closing had dislodged the gum to drop out of the ear.

He found tweezers and a sample jar in a sterile cabinet. He was uncertain if the gum would still have another person's DNA, but he remembered the ambiguity surrounding Hugh Rice's death and bottled the gum for testing.

Darcy was sure that the Gardai would show interest if the gum revealed DNA other than that of the corpse and sent the sample to the lab.

*Commander Dunlevy heard of the DNA find when he used his mobile to call his office at headquarters, as the ferry loaded for the run back to Ballymagilligan. The Gardai data base held the DNA profile of a Dolores Murphy. A colleague in his office told him that the Gardai had previously charged Dolores, and he had led the prosecution at the Summerhill district court. Dolly, as she was known, assaulted a woman, in a pub brawl, with fingernails, fists, pointed shoes and whirling handbag. The woman had suffered facial injuries: scratches, blackened eyes, loose teeth, and that skilled dental and plastic surgeons had returned her face to passable semblance of its former likeness. Wounds to her lower abdomen and legs had healed well. His successful prosecution of the case had resulted in Dolores' imprisonment for three months and a criminal record.

Dolores' DNA had a partial, familial match for that found on the gum.

It pointed to one or both of the Murphy girls being the suspects believed of being Hugh Rice's close companions when he succumbed, permanently, to their charms.

Dunlevy had previously thought long on what charge he could bring against the Murphy girls. He was no closer to a decision on hearing of the chewing gum and the findings. Apart from the trace of semen on the end of his penis, proving he had recently had sex, either with his hand or a companion, the DNA on the gum was the only evidence obtained from the body of Hugh Rice. The body had the appearance of having undergone a meticulous cleaning. A steward, no name given, had changed bed sheets before Gardai had visited the ferry, the linen, sent ashore for laundering, no longer available for testing. And it could be argued that the gum had been placed in the ear before the sandwich had taken place.

Was the DNA proof a Murphy girl had been a lover or both sisters had been his companions in the reported sandwich. The reference to Hugh being the meat in a sandwich an ambulance paramedic had picked up from a crew member's casual remark, on attending the call and uplifting Hugh from the ferry. The paramedics had looked for signs of life once Hugh was onboard the ambulance but he was gone.

The company Personnel Officer's only comment was that records showed purser Hugh Rice awarded the Murphy girls a larger overtime payments than what the other purser attached to the ferry did. The term screwing more overtime out of him the PO had also mentioned whilst almost collapsing in the throes of laughter.

Dunlevy decided he had to have a chat with the girls. They might reveal a felonious motive in their conduct with the Hugh Rice, though he was sure neither of them would admit wanting to shag him to death.

He would interview them individually on the return trip.

*Back in the office, Alf relieved from his duties, with nothing to report, Rupert picked up his mobile, sat down in the warm chair and switched it on, waited for it to kick into life. The bars appearing he found his wife's name in his contact list and called her number.

'Rupert how is the new job going?' were the first words Sophie spoke.

'It's certainly been different. I've had three day that have been more interesting than I ever experienced deep sea. You wouldn't believe the range of characters in the ferry crew, the onboard incidents, the sinister happenings, since I boarded last Wednesday. I'm sure it will all calm down and I'll be happy and have a worthwhile job. How have you been? Have you been away scrambling for Scrabble victories with your team?'

'Scrabble, yes. I was ready and dressed to go as my mobile started burring. A car has pulled up and is waiting outside. My companion for tonight, Marion, is driving me. It's her turn. We're off to play a friendly with the Carluke Lady Scrabblers. We've never played them before. It will be our most distant game if they join our SSB. I'll have to shoot now. We cannot arrive late. Have the other team waiting for us. Call me tomorrow morning if you get a chance, bye,' The line went dead.

Rupert clicked his mobile off, slumped back in his chair. Having learned a word or two of Irish parlance he mouthed 'feckin Scrabble', closed his eyes and pulled a bitter face. Irking his thoughts, making his body shake with anger, were when Sophie might have time for him, fancy making love to him again, his married life change, to a loving relationship, for the better, if ever!

He wasn't in the doldrums for too long, his thoughts subsided on returning to the duties expected of him. Passengers had begun to board, a queue forming at the hatch, all wanting Sterling changed into Euros. During his banking duties he'd heard the rumble of the main engines starting up and later felt the slight swell that told him the ferry had altered course for Ballymagilligan, having sailed beyond the breakwater.

By 20:30 hours the queue gone, he closed the hatch and left the office. Minded that he should check the owners suite so that he could tell Cara what she had to do to put it back in order, he decided to do that. Abi was taking a trip the following week to fit the new optics, whether he was still onboard or not, and would want the suite immaculate if she chose to stay overnight. He closed the hatch, locked up and headed for the engineer's alleyway and the upper deck.

He found the owner's suite unlocked and switched on the lights to look around. The bed linen would need changing. The waste bin had crumpled and torn up paper littering the bottom and needed emptying. The carpet had bits of fluff that a hoovering would remove. The bathroom didn't need a spring-clean, maybe a bog brush to clean the bowl, remove the tiny skidmark. All he had to do was tell Cara to put the suite back to normal.

At the foot of the stairs he noticed the officer's smoke room door open. He took a step to the side and looked in. He thought Dunlevy had recently arrived. Dunlevy turned, saw Rupert standing at the door and said, 'Come in, R.'

Rupert didn't know what he meant by calling him R but stepped inside and closed the door behind him.

Rupert saw the smug look on Dunlevy's face, as if he were taking the piss and knew he was when he said, repeating the R, 'Well R, what can I do you for?'

Irked already by the wife who couldn't take a minute or two out from her scrabble evening to have a decent conversation, Rubert felt an overwhelming rage well up inside him. What was the meaning of calling him R? 'What's with this R name calling,' he asked, his voice rising a decibel or two.

'Because it goes very well in front of Sewell,' Dunlevy replied, the smirk lingering. not leaving his face, adding to Rupert's growing anger. R Sewell! Instantly, Rupert knew what that sounded like.

Never in his life had he been so insulted. The tether on his anger burst asunder, making him take a step towards Dunlevy.

Irish sea navigators call the sensation, the slight lurch at the point where the vessel passes from the deep trench at the middle of the Irish Sea to shallower water as 'Crossing the border'. The crossing lurch occurred as Rupert's hands were down by his side. He readied them to hinder Dunlevy, who, not having the sea legs to counteract the sudden roll of the ferry, stumbled towards him. The only thought in Rupert's mind was to fend off the inevitable collision, push him back, steadying hands against his chest. His hands moved upwards quicker than he intended. The heel of both hands slid off Dunlevy's chest and with significant force thrusting them, struck the point of his chin a stunning blow. Rupert heard the crunch of bone as Dunlevy's neck snapped, saw his head rock back at a crazy angle, watched his body slump back against the bulkhead and sink onto the settee.

What the fuck have I done were the first words that jumped into Rupert's head as he looked down at the crumpled body. He leant forward and felt Dunlevy's neck searching for signs of a pulse, life. None found, he realised he had released a lethal blow, one he had learned as a university student at their martial arts club and had never considered that he might one day use. He fidgeted, his feet turning him in a circle, before calming, thinking. He reached out a hand and turned the latch on the door until hearing a click, locking it from the inside.

His eyes settled on the rectangular-shaped porthole. It had a leather strop attached to the moveable glass base with holes for fitting over a small button fitted to the bulkhead that provided a fixed level of opening. He saw it afforded space enough, when fully open, for a body of Dunlevy's slender bulk to easily pass through and fall directly into the sea. If he had the strength to move it.

He took the leather strop in hand and lowered the glass as quietly as he could to the fully open position. A gust of fresh and cold air blew around his head. With the crook of an arm between Dunlevy's legs he lifted. The body was heavier than he thought. He would have to try harder. Driven by anger and fear a mighty heave got it moving. He slid it up the bulkhead, his other hand lifting and guiding the head and shoulders through the porthole. Then with a push he jettisoned the body out into the dark night. He closed the porthole and breathed in deeply, his body shaking, his thoughts in turmoil. That he believed Dunlevy had called him an arsehole was not mitigating circumstances that a jury would ever accept!

Rupert wondered what Drake and Higson felt when they dispatched the chief cook over the side. At least a monk had saved their victim. He hoped Dunlevy would never be found. The two seamen were probably looking at attempted murder or endangering life, whilst he would face a murder charge, if caught and charged.

He had to leave quickly with no witnesses to his being anywhere near the smoke room and Dunlevy. If Dunlevy intended to continue interviewing crew then one of the remining onboard Gards could be on their way to the smokeroom with another interviewee. No one had seen him in or near the smokeroom or seen him near or in the owner's suite. He had to move quickly, away to another area of the ferry, unseen, to safety.

He looked around the smoke room. The recording equipment stood ready for use on a table, the switch in the off position. He took his handkerchief from a pocket and wiped the door lock as he turned it to open, whilst picturing in his mind the layout of the ferry, looking for the safest route to anywhere onboard other than where he was. The outside deck on the owner's suite level would take him aft to stairs leading down to the top freight deck.

His ear pressed against the door he listened for activity in the alleyway. Hearing none, he stepped out of the smokeroom, pulling the door closed behind him, and took to the stairs up. At the top of the stairs he heard the alleyway door open and voices. It was Screwfix and Bo. They had knocked off after stand-by in the engine room. He was lucky. He opened the side door to the open deck, closed the door quietly behind him and walked aft, took the stairs all the way down to the top freight deck. He walked along the length of the nearest alleyway until he came to the cross-alleyway and the galley. No one had seen him. The lights were still on in the galley. He walked in. Hamish stood at a work bench a pencil in his hand. He turned and said, 'Hello, Boss. I'll be with you in a second. I'm just jotting down tomorrow's menu choices. Of course, I've defrosted enough steaks for dinner to satisfy all concerned.'

'I'm sure you're on top of it all. Thought you might want to take me into your pig for a pint. I'm sure the commander will still be using ours for the remaining interviews he wants to do.'

'No problem, Boss,' Hamish said putting the pencil down, 'come with me. I'll lock up and have a pint with you.'

Log 3 of Hamish Macnab

The disappearance of Commander Dunlevy.

The Holigan Express was well on its way to the Port of Ballymagilligan that Saturday crossing from Holyhead. I had completed my galley duties and was sitting relaxing over a pint in the pig, along with the purser, Mr Sewell, who fancied a pint and couldn't use the officer's smoke room as the commander was using that facility to conduct his interviews.

The senior male Gard left onboard had not found Commander Dunlevy, where he expected him to find him, in the officer's smokeroom. The interview of other crew members should have begun, the Gard to usher the crewmembers the commander still wished to interview, including the Murphy sisters, individually, to the smoke room for their interview with the commander. The Gard's search of passenger spaces had not located the commander. The officer on watch on the bridge had not seen the commander recently and had no idea where he could be either but he alerted the captain to the situation. Captain Davies had not seen the commander since dinner. The ferry was now an hour away from the Irish coast. The captain ordered crew to search the ferry. If the search did not find the commander on board, turning the ferry to search the sea was a choice he thought unproductive: It was a pitch black night with limited visibility.

Suggestions the Gard heard for his commander's non-appearance on asking, from the two female Gards, and the off duty crew relaxing in the pig, ranged from a jocular, inevitable, turfing 'into the drink' to him going walkabout ashore in Holyhead. The walk ashore sighting was unconfirmed by any Gard.

'Missing the ship', as the mariner's saying goes, and making his way back to the republic by a different route was a suggestion, discussed at length by Gards, that could explain the commander's disappearance but the majority felt it unlikely. However discussions did include his going ashore, losing his way, couldn't find his way back to the Holigan Express, had walked too far, couldn't get back before the ferry sailed, and was now on different company's ferry on his way to Dublin by that route. Briefly, they discussed the possibility that something sinister might have happened to him on his walk ashore.

I later learned that the Chief officer, in charge of the vehicle loading couldn't say the commander hadn't gone ashore. His duties took him other parts of the decks and ashore during the loading.

Both the purser Rupert Sewell and I told the senior Gard that we had not seen the commander; the purser since he left the saloon after dinner, he busy, after dinner, in his office changing Sterling to Euros for passengers. I had not left the galley since the ferry docked in Holyhead.

The search continued when the ferry docked in Ballymagilligan, disrupting crewmember's ideas of a run ashore to the pub for a pint. The captain ordered all crewmembers to complete the search to a conclusion.

The purser joined me in searching catering storerooms and fridge spaces. After an hour, the chief officer confirmed to the captain that the commander was definitely not onboard.

The senior Gard had contacted Inspector Power as the ferry neared the Irish coast and the availability of a mobile signal. Inspector Power rejoined the ferry when the ferry docked. Power and the Gard found the commander's Audi Quattro parked and locked close to the ferry company booking office.

The mystery deepened. All lorries, cars and passengers had left the ferry when the inspector returned to the area where the commander had parked the car to find it missing. The female Gard, on duty at the stern ramp, the only way off the ferry by foot, reported that no crew had left the ferry when the foot passengers disembarked. No office personnel saw the car leave the parking area.

Power requested and received the names of all travelling passengers and lorry drivers on board that crossing. Worryingly, two lorry drivers were known to the Gardai, had form, arrested in the past by a squad led by the commander for drug possession and had done time. Inspector Power told me that the lorry drivers were the main persons of interest, they unable to provide unshakeable alibis for their time onboard the ferry and after driving their lorries off onto the dock area. On the lorry's arrival at their depots, Gardai had been waiting. A search of the lorries provided no clues that might explain the commander's disappearance; however, searchers found, attached to the underside of each lorry, a 20 kilo stash of cocaine. The Gardai detained the drivers in custody for further questioning.

On leaving the ferry on my final day on board, the Gardai had not found the commander or his car. The inspector told me that the Gardai knew that Audis and other expensive makes were prime targets for the Republic's criminal gangs, that they broke them down into spare parts and shipped them in containers to African and Caribbean ports. The inspector also revealed to me his thoughts that the commander's mysterious disappearance would become one of the very few unsolved cases on the Gardai books.

In retrospect, working 12 hours a day, longer if you are the only cook, in a ship's galley is the wrong place to investigate crimes committed elsewhere onboard. However, being a detective I am extremely irked that I was unable to lay a hand on a shoulder and utter the words 'you're nicked' to a culprit, and I'm sure Inspector Power of the Gardai feels the same.

EPILOGUE

Drake and Higson.

Inspector Power led the prosecution of the two seamen on a charge under the Irish Republic Offences Against The Person Act. The evidence of Sean Fleck's belt found in the pocket of Higson's donkey jacket, the most conclusive piece of evidence against them, backed the sworn statements of the Gards who arrested and sat with Drake in his cabin and heard his confession. Both Drake and Higson had pleaded guilty. Considering the facts of the case the judge sentenced each to five years in prison. They both hope, in time, that the Irish Government would allow their exchange for two Irish prisoners serving time in Liverpool's Walton Gaol. With remission for good behaviour release could come after serving four years.

Purser Rupert Sewell.

Rupert continued his career as purser with the Holigan Ferry Company. He has not yet bedded Abi, though the hint it might be an easy conquest has not diminished. Abi has suggested that they meet the day before he rejoins the ferry for a night in a hotel close to the train station in Warrington, where he would change trains. Life at home increasing his frustrations, 'yon' still not on the cards, Rupert has not ruled out the tryst. His wife thinks him grumpy, his take on her scrabble fixation unchanged.

No crew member has called him 'R' or 'Lucky', the utterances of the letter or the word likely to irk him to an overwhelming irritability.

Detective Constable Hamish MacNab.

Hamish returned to detective duties with the Met at the end of his week onboard with unbelievable stories to tell his colleagues. Commander Dewsnap did not tell Hamish he was pleased to see him back. Didn't tell him he was impressed with the results of his week cruising, as he put it, but circumstances as they were and his extra galley work, he understood why Hamish only had limited success.

Tara and Cara Murphy.

Inspector Power has not interviewed Tara and Cara, quizzed them over their relationship with Hugh Rice and how he died. That one or the other found a handy receptacle for a wad of well-chewed gum did not constitute a cause of death, perhaps only a sudden loss of hearing. He does not expect the sisters or any crew member to admit having knowledge of how or why the commander disappeared. No crewmembers heard the private conversation between Tara and Cara, on learning of the commander's disappearance. Tara said, 'I hope he's been feckin decked and ditched, never to be feckin found.'

Cara replying, 'And feckin good riddance to the bastard! I hope I never see the fecker's face again.'

The sisters continue to work on the ferry doing the same jobs. They have not had their wicked way with purser Rupert Sewell. Seeing no encouraging signs, they are still a hundred Euros a month short from what their earlier pay packets were, under, or alongside, knowledgeable crewmembers have said, purser Hugh Rice, who paid them for fictitious overtime and very generous it was, to be sure.

Sean Fleck continues to cook for hungry Gards at the local Gardai station. The company employed a chief cook with competency in colcannon and coddle cooking from an Irish marine employment agency. They promoted Tommy to the position of second cook.

This is a Fairy Story

Liar of the Year

Robbie Beaghan won the All Ireland Liar of the Year Contest for 57 years on-the-belt-end. Held in the Navigator's Den public house, in the small town of Ballyfallacy, he'd thrashed all purveyors of untruths. In those years, no contestant outlied him. Although renowned and feted as the best liar that the island of Ireland had ever produced, he knew fibbers with potential, lurking in the wings, were dreaming up fictions, honing their fables, waiting for him to falter. He always had to have a better fib to impress the wise men judging the competition and this year again, he was sure, he had the best lie ever told.

Both Robbie and his wife Molly were 78 years old. Molly had remonstrated to Robbie since his last conquest that it was time to quit the competition. 57 years of winning the same prize, a fortnight holidaying in a horse-drawn, gypsy caravan in County Donegal, had become both tedious and painful. Her ageing backside had suffered the buffeting of potholed country tracks in the unsprung vehicles. The jig jogging mulish, surly brutes between the shafts, masquerading as horses, never seemed to miss a rut or boulder and she didn't wish to suffer it all again.

The couple had circumnavigated the peaty waters of Lough Veagh 57 times, plodded through the forty shades of greenery of the Veagh national park, back and forth, 114 times. Molly had watched Robbie gaze in awe for hours at flat topped Muckish mountain, 57 times, whilst bottoming a bottle of Old Paddy Whiskey. A part of the prize, the whiskey had done nothing to assuage the pain in Molly's backside or for her to show any love for equines. The very word assuage, in her mind, meant she was blameworthy for the old flab hanging from her backside.

For his 58th and consecutive entry into the competition, Robbie had a blockbuster of a lie to tell. He'd told Molly often enough during the months preceding the competition that he would be unbeatable once more, for sure. Not privy to Robbie's thinking, but sure that he'd never dare fib to her, Molly visited the contest pub to view their notice board. Rumours abounded that, this year, alternative prizes were available for the victor to choose. And so it was. They offered a prize that would please her: a Divan Suite. She'd insist he accept that prize instead of choosing to undertake another arduous, pony-drawn, painful excursion around County Donegal. Lie to her, would he?

The highlight of the 11th of July that year, as it had been since 1906, in that part of the Island of Ireland, was The Liar of the Year Contest. Liar fans had been arriving at the venue since opening time, the younger element becoming inebriated, singing morbid songs un-melodiously by the time the competition got underway. Most attendees were Robbie fans who were rigidly ignoring the fabrications of early contestants. Robbie's fans stood out by an Irish mile. All had dressed in the bib and tucker of the Irish labourer: the donkey jacket. Wearers had smartened up the attire with a black, string tie hanging from the collar of a white, nylon shirt.

The concert hall filled as Robbie's time approached. When the stage and hall lighting dimmed, and the spotlight above the competitor's entrance blazed into life, all knew his appearance was nigh. Onto the stage, an assistant carried the 'Lying Down Pouffe' stuffed with duck feathers and down. The establishment only allowed earlier winners of the competition to park their backside on this leather-bound bag, and so it had been since 1906.

Robbie, with a twinkle in both eyes, slid through the competitor's entrance sideways to rapturous applause and danced an impromptu jig as he took to the steps leading to the stage. When the curtains opened and the stage lights went up, Robbie was sitting cross-legged, recumbent on the pouffe.

When the shouts of 'Make it a good one Robbie,' and the hand clapping died, Robbie raised both arms for complete quiet, then he began his lie in his eloquent, Cork accent.

THE LIE

Before the advent of the spade, but when the shovel was still the favoured tool of skilled navvies, the itinerant, tin pot teapot repairman and provider of illegal herbs, known as Shifty, made an earth-shattering discovery. Shifty lived in that hard to pinpoint mobile hamlet, with the ever-changing postcode, Randomtown. He was sitting up front of the leading caravan of the train, heading again for that night's stop at Randomtown. The night parking always had to offer a clean water supply and a wide tree to provide screened toilet facilities at the back of. All the trees at the stops, tall and broad of trunk, had growth nutrients provided in abundance over the years.

Alongside him sat his thick-hipped wife, Rosehip. Rosehip's given name was O'Hipps and Shifty had rescued her from a travelling circus that displayed her great arse as a national treasure.

Shifty was puffing away merrily at his long-stemmed clay pipe, the smoke keeping at bay clegs and midges that found his face more attractive than the pony's arse. He was gazing over the swishing tail and bobbing head of his pony when he saw a sneeze approaching along a track leading into a small wood. He would have seen it much earlier had he been looking towards the copse. He never liked the way he'd heard the word pronounced, thought it had portent for all dodgy dealers, never used the word himself in case it provoked a visit from the Gardai. In shock, his teeth clamped down on the pipe stem, shattering it. He spat the pieces out and shouted loudly, 'Heavens to O'Bloody Murgatroyd, I've just spotted something very interesting and I don't think it a parablepsis!'

'A para what? What in the name o' the big man is one o' those?' Rosehip screeched deafeningly into Shifty's nearest ear.

'Tis mysterious, for sure, but I believe my eyes. As soon as I saw the sneeze, it disappeared. One of the little people was standing on the same spot. Knee high to a grasshopper, he was, to be sure and wearing a wee suit of clothing. Then the sneeze was back again, for a split second, ephemeral like, about as long as a rat's fart would hang about in a wind tunnel. Then the wee fellah reappeared on the same spot. The wee fellah's gone again now and so is the sneeze. Begorrah an' Bejasus, that imp or leprechaun, whatever it was, but I'm sure it wasn't a banshee for I heard no wailing, must have gone through a bodily turmoil to pull off that trick, to be sure. Must have been a fierce sternutation. A sneeze of brobdingnagian proportions. A massive constuperation of his thropple to have caused that!'

'You're talkin' baloney again, to be sure you are, if you expect me to believe a tale the likes o' that. Brobdingnagian, you say. What kind of word is that? Never heard the likes,' Rosehip responded, sagely nodding her head.

'Tis a big word from Gulliver's Travels that you wouldn't know about, to be sure,' Shifty answered.

In his role as mobile herbalist, Shifty had listened to his customers tell of the magical concoction that only the little people had. Rumour had spread that, when taken as a snuff, it enabled the little people to disappear in a sneezing fit when danger loomed.

Shifty had nothing as potent in his pharmacy, but he could see advantages in the ability to disappear. He could create a market for such a substance. Members of the caravan train disappeared under cover of darkness on a wild night, to return with eggs and chickens stolen from farmers' coops. He could change that into a daytime dodge for them. Rogues, who wished, together with any stolen loot carried, to vanish before the law could put a hand on a shoulder, would be his best customers.

Shifty needed to source or discover the recipe for this explosive snuff. He needed to capture one of the little people but had no idea how. For months, he kept his ear to the ground listening for another sneezing fit that would produce on the other side of the fierce sternutation a trappable imp.

It was as the sun was quarter up that day when Shifty heard it. He was lying awake in the quiet of the Randomtown morning, alongside Rosehip, who had ceased her morning, heroic-snoring display that had rabbits crapping themselves, scurrying for their warrens. The staccato, reverberating sound must have come from elsewhere. He clambered out of the caravan onto the driving seat and listened intently. He heard it again, a sound like none he'd ever heard: a sneeze, a cough, then a sneeze again then a strangulated cough and a sneeze rolled into one. Surely this was an imp of an odd sort, one who sounded distressed, wasn't in the best of health; an imp that would be easier to trap than a healthy, disappearing-in-a-flash one. Tracing the sound as coming from the steep hill to the east, Shifty quickly dressed and made his way towards the slopes, homing in on the sound.

He rounded a bend in the track and saw it. No bigger than a tall standing grasshopper was the wee fella. Shifty could see the imp and the imp could see Shifty. The imp began to shake, seemingly trying to conjure up a sneezing fit, which would cause his disappearance. Shifty started to run towards the imp, reaching it whilst stooping low. With an outstretched hand, he grabbed it, before any vanishing act could take place.

His hand tight around the wriggling creature, Shifty stuffed it into a fob pocket, which at once began to leap about, a bit like a madly palpitating ticker. In a final, sudden mad lunge of desperation, the imp leapt at the fob lining, then all activity ceased.

Shifty raced back to the caravan. Inside, he shook Rosehip to wakefulness, which was never an easy task. 'I've captured an Imp,' he cried out in delight and started to fumble with finger and thumb into the fob.

'What twaddle are you quoting to me now, you dolt,' Rosehip responded loudly.

Shifty lifted out of the fob pieces of a miniscule man.

'To be sure and Bejasus it looks like pieces of a rattly old Hillman Imp, to me,' Rosehip roared her assessment of the discovery.

Groping deep in the fob, Shifty produced what he'd hoped to find: it was a tiny pouch, a scrotum sac that a gelder had skilfully sliced from a toad. He hoped, in the tiny receptacle, a toad's scrotum, he would find the miraculous snuff. First, he had to assess any contents. He looked at Rosehip. Yes, she would be the ideal guinea pig and if anything untoward happened to her, he would gain the space on the driving seat that her great arse occupied and have no loud, annoying cackle in his ears. A tincture or two remained in the pouch. Taking a pinch and laying it in a line on the back of his hand, Shifty offered it up to Rosehip's nose, and said, 'Here, take a goodly sniff at this.'

More compliant than usual, Rosehip consented and took a long inhalation, vacuuming the pinch into the upper reaches of her nasal cavity. The reaction of her body to the snuff was mind blowing. In the midst of an onrush of a humungous sneeze that would never reach fruition, the top of Rosehip's head shot off, spinning horizontally, creating a hole in the roof of the caravan as neat as any skilled cabinetmaker could carve with a fret saw.

Today, all caravans have this addition. Travellers fitting the stack of a stove through the handy gap have smoke free, indoor cooking facilities and central heating.

'Supporters, whether you believe me or not, that is the last lie you'll hear me tell,' Robbie ended his 58th lie.

Robbie admirers, who had stood in rapt silence, in respect, and to perfectly hear his words, missing nothing of the lie, erupted in cheering. The judges, fearing a dousing in the nearby stream had they voted otherwise, raised Robbie's arms high as the victor of the contest. All agreed: his lie was the best by an Irish mile.

Molly was standing on the home doorstep and in earshot of the adulation that she expected to erupt inside the pub. She smiled and turned as the roar hit her hearing, then scurried quickly though the house to the back yard. In a pile, she's stacked the old family seating that she expected Robbie's prize to replace. Liberally sprinkled with paraffin, the pile burst into flame as the match made contact.

An hour later, Robbie and a posse of inebriated supporters helped him cart the diving suit that Molly so desired. Today, viewers can see the suit standing, filled with cement and stiffly erect, in the corner of Robbie's garden.

The note hanging around its neck states: This is my tribute to all women who think they know best!

Signed,

Robbie Beaghan.

Printed in Great Britain
by Amazon